KAUMUALI'I AND THE LAST OF HAWAII'S GOD KINGS

BY:

LEE B. CROFT

SPHYNX PUBLICATIONS
PHOENIX, ARIZONA, USA

MMXVII
2017

© **COPYRIGHT LEE B. CROFT, 2017**
ALL RIGHTS RESERVED WORLDWIDE
No part of this book may be reproduced, stored in a retrieval system, or transmitted by any means without the written permission of the author.

Sphynx Publications is located at 11622 S. Tusayan Ct., Phoenix, Arizona 85044 USA. Telephone is 480-567-4501. Email to Lbcroft@cox.net
ISBN 978-0-9985627-2-8

The author of this book, Lee B. Croft (1946—), Ph.D., is a teacher, scholar, and Professor Emeritus of the Russian Language and Culture at Arizona State University, where he taught and administered language programs for thirty-eight years (1973-2011). He is the author of 16 books and over 300 scholarly articles, translations, and reviews, several of which involve relation of Hawaiian history. He has been a part-time resident of Hawaii (O'ahu and Kaua'i) for more than thirty years and is an associate of Kaua'i's "Friends of King Kaumuali'i" (see http://kauaikingkaumualii.org)

Cover portrait by Brook Kapūkuniahi Parker, 2012

Introduction

The ruling ali'i (nobility and royalty) of the Hawaiian islands were not just kings, but god kings, claiming by genealogical connection to their ancestral gods an actual divinity which dramatically colored their relationships with each other and with their people. In the god-king polity that evolved in this highly spiritual culture, the ruling elite sometimes acted in ways that we in our modern civilization might arrogantly consider reprehensible. Yet as the Hawaiian people's common soul merged into a more global mass consciousness, its basic humanity shined through the elite minority's obsessive severity to illumine everyone's days together in what is now called the Aloha Spirit. After the death of the unifying King Kamehameha I in 1819, the succeeding ali'i voluntarily deactivated their claims of divinity and reformed their conception of monarchy. The last to do this—after Liholiho, Ka'ahumanu, Keōpūolani, and even Kalanimoku, was King Kaumuali'i of Kaua'i, whose reasons for surrendering his divinity were the loftier aspects of his humanity—a desire for peace and justice—gained from his mother's parenthood and from the influence of foreigners with whom he had deliberately learned to converse. He really wanted his people to have better lives…to be educated, to live Aloha…on already paradisiacal Kaua'i. This, the triumph of his evolved humanity over a claim of divinity, is why Kaumuali'i deserves memorialization. — LBC.

Acknowledgements: Dr. Lesley Hoyt Croft, *Tammi Andersland, Dr. John Lydgate, Barbara Bennett, Aletha Goodwin Kaohi, Carrie Newcombe, Carol Hart, Brook Kapūkuniahi Parker, Reg Gage, Shirley and David Dauterman, *Herb Kawainui Kāne, Raymond A. Massey, *Richard A. Pierce, Peter H. Hempfling, Maureen Fodale, Dr. B. Ka'imiloa Chrisman, Patricia Polansky, Bill and Judy Fernandez, Stu Burley. These are the names of some of the people who helped me create this book, but only I am responsible for any shortcomings of it.   *=passed.   —LBC.

Kaumuali'i and the Last of Hawaii's God Kings

by:

Lee B. Croft

HABITATION OF HAWAII: WHO, FROM WHERE AND BY WHEN:

Two recent books which apply twenty-first century science to the history of Hawaii are Anthropologist Patrick Vinton Kirch's <u>A Shark Going Inland Is My Chief: The Island Civilization of Ancient Hawai'i</u> [1] and Oceanographer Richard W. Grigg's <u>In the Beginning—ARCHIPELAGO—The Origin and Discovery of the Hawaiian Islands</u>.[2] These authors, both life-long members of the Hawaiian "'ohana" (family), have added much to our understanding of Hawaii's human habitation and its development of a unique and fascinating civilization. These works generally agree that Hawaii, certainly one of the world's most isolated inhabited places, received its first human settlers more recently than was previously thought. Carbon dating of ash from the hearths of the earliest known habitations generally do not precede 800 AD, nor do any known relics. It is possible that the first humans to discover the Hawaiian islands

---

[1] Kirch 2012 in Bibliography.

[2] Grigg 2012 in Biblio.

came from the Marquesas and the Society islands no earlier than that, though some would disagree. These first settlers were the inheritors of the Lapita culture of Southeast Asia that migrated into the Pacific between 1500 and 1200 BC. By the time they inhabited Polynesia they had mastered ocean travel in sail-and-paddle-propelled double-hulled canoes that could sustain their crews for many months of open-sea sailing. Their mastery of navigation by natural signs (stars, clouds, winds, sea flotsam, birds…) to achieve such travel has been well demonstrated by the replica double-hulled canoe *Hōkūle'a*.

It may surprise many to learn that in defining the time period of Hawaiian habitation there is in most cases really not a conflict between the datings of modern science and the datings of the preliterate Hawaiian culture's own oral historians. Indeed in some instances the oral historians and the scientists are in substantive agreement about the time and the origins of Hawaiian habitation. Kaua'i historian Frederick B. Wichman, in his Nā Pua Ali'i o Kaua'i: Ruling Chiefs of Kaua'i,[3] gives a superb picture of how the Hawaiian oral historians… mostly the "kahuna" (priests) of the Hawaiian religion…used memorized chants to trace their rulers' genealogy back to their gods. These chants bring to mind the Christian culture's "Biblical 'Begats',"

---

[3] Wichman 2003.

recanting the genealogy of Jesus back in time to the Old Testament patriarch Abraham.[4] The particular chant that Wichman chooses to analyze is called the "Kumu-honua Genealogy," taking the Proto-Polynesians' first man ("Kumu-honua") and first woman ("Lalo-honua") through 36 generations of specified descendents, across 925 years (counting 25 years per "generation"), until back at generation 37 we have "Papa-nui-hānau-moku," (called for short "Papa") the "earth mother progenitor of the Polynesian people" and her husband "Wakea."

Papa was thought to live in Fiji, Samoa, or Tonga, and she led her people further eastward into the vast Pacific Ocean, where her descendent people "discovered the famed islands of the South Pacific: Nukuhiwa, Ra'iātea, Tahiti, and, in time, the islands of the Hawaiian Archipelago." Wichman then elaborates on a "Broken Genealogy" which explains the origins of Hawaii's "menehune" people who descended separately from "Ka-lani-menehune," who was recited at genealogy position number 24 in the descendancy from Kumu-honua to Papa. The "Nana-'ulu Genealogy" then lists the descendants of Papa and Wakea for 13 generations to "Ki'i," who was a Prince of Tahiti. His son "Nana-'ulu sailed north and found the Hawaiian islands, which were already settled by people

---

[4] Howard 2013.

claiming descent from Ka-lani-menehune. They had already settled Nihoa, Necker, Ni'ihau, and Kaua'i."

Another 26 generations list the ruling descendants of Ki'i to La'a-mai-kahiki. By Wichman's count of 25-year generations back from the known genealogy of Kauai's rulers, he gives the estimated European calendar date of Ki'i's Tahitian rule at 830 AD,[5] his son Nana-ulu's arrival in the Hawaiian islands at ca. 875 AD, and of La'a-mai-kahiki's rule on Kaua'i as 1305-1330 AD.[6] So, we can see that the conclusions made as a result of modern science— comparative linguistics, human genetics, carbon dating of hearths and artifacts, and palynology (layers of plant pollens in earth strata)— affirm some of the preliterate Hawaiian chants about the origins of their islands' habitation—**who** (the Lapita people), **where** (from Southeast Asia through Polynesia, especially Tahiti and the Marquesas) and **when** (possibly as late as ca. 875 AD). A similar reconciliation between scientific dating and oral history may be seen for O'ahu in Cordy.[7]

---

[5] Wichman 2003, p. 137.

[6] Ibid. p. 139.

[7] Cordy 2002, p. 12, then Note 10, p. 51.

DEVELOPMENT OF A CIVILIZATION: GODS AND KAPUS:

By 1000 AD more than one canoe had followed the original discoverers to the Hawaiian islands and for four hundred years thereafter there was probably intermittent two-way communication between the residents of the Hawaiian islands and at least the Society Islands, particularly Tahiti. The languages of the Hawaiians and the Tahitians are clearly related. But then this communication ceased during the last four hundred years before western contact (i.e. from about 1400 to 1778),[8] leaving the Hawaiian islands in striking isolation from contact with other societies.

In this isolation the Hawaiian residents evolved a distinct society with its political structure changing from hereditary chiefs to kings to "god kings" who integrated their identities into the polytheistic animist religion and enforced a series of behavioral restrictions called "kapus" (taboos) on their subjects some of which were enforceable by death. There were hundreds of deities in the Hawaiian native religion, but the most important ones, to which "heiaus" (temples) and "ki'i" (wooden idols) were most often erected and maintained are: Kāne (sunlight, water, the creation of animals and man), Lono (agriculture, rain, fitness, healing), Kū (war

---

[8] See Kirch 2012, pp. 124-126.

and numerous kinds of husbandry and crafts), and Kanaloa (ocean, ocean winds, companion of Kāne). Among the lesser deities are Pele (female demigod, goddess of volcanoes and fire), Kamapua'a (male demigod of fertile lands, and both consort and antagonist of Pele), and Laka (female demigod and goddess of Hula).

Some of the kapus were protective of the environment, like those prohibiting the commoners from fishing in especially productive places which were strictly reserved to the "ali'i" (nobility, including the god kings). Dr. Grigg argues that such kapus had an important ecological function that became imperative when the Hawaiian population reached its peak (estimated to 400,000 and more) in the 17th century.[9] This population surpassed the ability of natural resources to sustain it, both stressing the land environment and causing a subsequent human population decline. But from the work of Dr. Kirch, who uses the shark as a metaphor for the ali'i, one could easily conclude that this population decline may also have been a direct consequence of the rivalries among the island ali'i, who set about to conquer the others by warring on them, killing people in great numbers.[10]

---

[9] Grigg 2012, p. 2. and Bushnell 1993, pp. 115-183.

[10] Kirch 2012, p. 2, Ridley 2010, p. 262, and also Kamakau 1992, pp. 235-237.

Other kapus were gender discriminational, like the " 'ai kapu" (eating taboo) prohibiting women from eating with men and prohibiting women and girls from eating a long list of available dietary items…bananas, coconuts, and pork, for example. And all the food was prepared by the men only. Women were considered potentially defiling of mens' work, weapons, etc. by dint of the blood of menstruation, and when they were menstruating they were restricted in separate houses. Men and women did not sleep together unless involved in procreation but lived in separated quarters built by the males only. But others of the kapus had no apparent clear purpose. The most egregious of these was the "prostration kapu" demanding that commoners lie down and put their faces into the ground whenever they encountered the presence of a "kapu moe" (possessing the prostration kapu) ali'i.

Here are some excerpts from how David Malo in his Hawaiian Antiquities: Mo'olelo Hawai'i described "The Ali'i and the Common People:" "…The great chiefs were entirely exclusive, being hedged about with many tabus (i.e. kapus… author), and a large number of people were slain for breaking, or infringing upon, these tabus. The tabus that hedged about an ali'i were exceedingly strict and severe…if the shadow of a man fell upon the house of a tabu chief, that man must be put to death, and so with anyone whose shadow fell upon the back of a chief, or upon his robe, or his malo ('loincloth'), or upon anything that belonged to the chief. If anyone passed through the private doorway of a tabu chief, or climbed over the stockade about his residence, he was put to death...If a man entered the ali'i's house without changing his wet malo, or with his head smeared with mud, he was put to death. Even if there were no fence surrounding the ali'i's residence, but only a mark or faint scratch in the ground hidden in the grass, and a man were to overstep this line unwittingly, not seeing it, he would be put to death...When a tabu chief ate, the people in his presence must kneel, and if anyone raised his knee from the ground, he was put to death. If any man put forth in a kioloa (long, narrow) canoe at the same time as the tabu chief, the penalty was death...If anyone girded himself with the king's malo, or put on the king's robe, he was put to death. There were many other tabus, some of them relating to the man and some to the king, for violating which anyone would be put to death."[11]

GOD KINGS AND HUMAN SACRIFICING:

For the first few hundred years of Hawaiian habitation, no humans were sacrificed and the chiefs could be supplanted by the people they ruled

---

[11] Malo 1997, p. 57.

if their rule did not satisfy the people.[12] But during the 14th century there arrived on the big island of Hawai'i a high priest named Pā'ao, perhaps Tahitian, who was outraged at the lack of respect from the people that the Hawaiian ali'i commanded. He summoned from his homeland an "ariki" (notice the linguistic similarity to "ali'i") war chief named Pilika'aiea ("Pili"), and together they built the first "luakini heiaus" (temples which included human sacrifice) at Mo'okini and elsewhere on Hawai'i island whose rituals dedicated to the god Kū as war god involved human sacrifices.[13] Pā'ao, Pili, and their successors managed, initially by force, to convince the people that these sacrifices pleased the gods so that the gods then protected them from natural disasters (hurricanes, volcanic eruptions, etc.), accidental deaths (shark attacks, etc.), famine, illness, or slaughter by other chiefs. Their genealogical chants mentioned in almost every generation some supernatural event wherein a predecessor's spiritual power spared the ruled population from all manner of damage and harm. People who resisted this belief were potentially subject to sacrifice or simply an abrupt death. These new ali'i demanded respect, then reverence, even adoration until they were literally worshipped by their subjects in an ever growing number of prescribed rituals.

---

[12] Kirch 2012, p. 204.

[13] Burgess/MacGowan 2000 and Kawaharada 2010

The sacrificing of humans came to be tolerated by the individuals in the population as essential to their mass welfare…it was thought to be the "responsibility" of the ali'i to keep them all safe. By 1700 AD, human sacrifice was taking place on all the Hawaiian islands[14] as the ali'i chiefs warred

The execution of a "prostration kapu" violator, by Jacques Arago, from: http://en.wikipedia.org/wiki/Jacques_Arago. Arago was in Hawaii, 1819.

with each other for inter-island supremacy. Each island ali'i desired that his "mana" (spiritual pow-

---

[14] Cordy 2002, Note 12, pp. 51-52.

er) was to become the only mana… and that all other ali'i genealogical lines…meaning the rival chiefs and all his relatives and subordinate chiefs be killed. Some might be sacrificed to the gods.

Execution of a Kapu violator by strangling (Maniere d'etranger un coupable aux iles Sandwich) by Jacques Etienne Arago (1790-1855), from: http://www.alamy.com by license.

The three main means of bringing about the death of a kapu violator or of an enemy chief or warrior were: striking or piercing the victim with a weapon, strangling the victim with a fiber rope, or drowning (clubbing or the latter two methods for sacrifices—there should be no blood). Occasionally execution even involved placing the victim (sometimes alive) into an earth oven.

By the time of western contact (British Captain James Cook's third voyage to the Pacific in 1778-9) control of all the major eight (8) inhabited Hawaiian islands were in the hands of THREE competing ali'i genealogical lines: the Hawai'i line of King Kamehameha going back to Pā'ao and further, who had eliminated all rival ali'i on the big island of Hawai'i (1); the Maui line of King Kahekili of Maui (2), Ka'aholawe (3), Moloka'i (4), and Lana'i (5); and the O'ahu (6) line of King Pele'ioholani, claimed by his heir Kaneoneo. Both the O'ahu line and the Maui line were represented

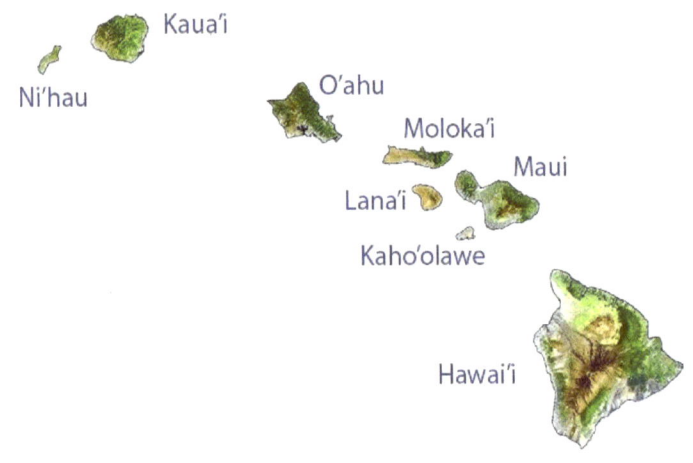

This map of the eight main inhabited Hawaiian islands is from www.statesymbolsusa.org.

by the wife-and-husband pair of Kaua'i (7) and Ni'ihau's (8) ruling ali'i, Kamakahelei and Ka'eokulani.

BIRTH SITE AND NAME OF KAUMUALI'I:

Most (but not all) historical sources agree that Kaua'i's last independent King, Kaumuali'i, (the 23rd hereditary "ali'i nui" of Kaua'i, Ni'ihau, and

These are the "Birthstones" at the Holoholoku Heiau in Wailua ahupua'a on Kaua'i where Kaumuali'i was born in 1780. Photo by Lee B. Croft in July 2014.

irregularly populated Lehua), was born at the start of the Hawaiian Makahiki season (late October or early November...the time involving the sight above the eastern horizon at sunset of the constellation Pleiades (Hawaiian "makali'i")) of our year 1780 at the Birthstones of the Holoholoku Heiau above the banks of the Wailua River on Kaua'i's eastern shore.[15] His mother, Kaua'i's distinquished ruling chiefess, Kamakahelei, announced his name accompanying the sound of the nearby "Bell Rock" as "Ka-umu-ali'i," meaning "the oven of the nobility," signifying her prediction that he would become "the means of nourishment" of Kaua'i's people. His father, Ka'eokulani, a high ali'i of the Maui line, favored another, more martial, rationale for his son's name, telling his chiefs that Kaumuali'i would become the conqueror of the other islands' rulers, sacrificing his ali'i rivals by roasting them in his namesake "oven of the nobility."[16]

---

[15] See Ho'omanawanui 2012, pp. 220-223.

[16] Zambucka 1999, p. 26.

KAUMUALI'I'S MOTHER AND HER HUSBANDS:

Kamakahelei, who was descended from the line of O'ahu chiefs[17] had children with three husbands of successively more powerful "mana," meaning "spiritual power" derived from a genealogical connection to the "akua" or gods. These husbands were, first, Ni'ihau Chieftain Kina (or "Kuina," or "Kiha") from about 1765 (he died in a battle against Kaneoneo's warriors on Ni'ihau about 1770); second, O'ahu ali'i Kaneoneo (grandson of Pele'ioholani and claimant to O'ahu rule through his deposed father Kūmahana); and lastly, after 1777, Ka'eokulani, half-brother of the ali'i nui Kahekili (Kahekilinuiahumanu... "feather cloaked mighty thunderer"), ruler until 1794 of the Maui Federation (the islands of Maui, Kaho'olawe, Moloka'i, Lana'i, and O'ahu) and son of Maui ruler Kekaulike, progenitor of many powerful ali'i.

The "mana" of some of these "ali'i" enabled the possession by some of them of the "kapu moe" (prostrating taboo) meaning that any commoners they encountered were required, under penalty of immediate death, to lie down and put their faces into the ground while in the ali'i's presence. The penalties for violation of this Hawaiian

---

[17] Wichman 2003, pp. 92-93 and p.129, also Buyers' site.

"kapu" (taboo) was carried out by the ali'i's accompanying "mū" (bodyguards) who went before them shouting announcement of their coming and indicating the sanctity with their kapu staves having highly visible white tapa balls atop them.

Kamakaheilei's three husbands—Kina, Kaneoneo, and Ka'eokulani— gave her at least six daughters and two sons.[18] The last husband, nine-years-younger Ka'eokulani, known as "Ka'eo," was a tall and very strong man, known as a particularly formidable warrior who strode fearlessly to meet adversaries with two ferocious "man-eating" mastiff dogs.[19]

Ka'eo and Kamakaheilei were the Kaua'i-ruling ali'i who were paddled out in a long double-hulled canoe to make first contact with English Captain James Cook and his men on the ships *Resolution* and *Discovery*, which anchored offshore at Waimea village on Kaua'i's south shore on January 19, 1778.[20]

---

[18] Croft 2012B, p. 359, also Wichman 2003, p. 92, and Kekoolani and Buyers.

[19] Daws 1974, p. 37.

[20] Massey 2009, historical painting on p. 21.

FIRST CONTACT WITH EUROPEAN CIVILIZATION— CAPT. COOK:

Seminal Hawaiian historian Samuel M. Kamakau, in his Ruling Chiefs of Hawaii, records the historic encounter between the native Hawaiians and the British Pacific explorers from the Hawaiian point of view. He relates that the first named brave Hawaiians who were given the assignment of climbing aboard Captain Cook's ship *Resolution* were Ka'eo's and Kamakahelei's chieftain Kaneakaho'owaha, their kahuna (priest) Kū'ohu, and their most formidable mu (bodyguard) Ki'ikīkī.[21] These three heroes were commissioned to determine if the British newcomers were gods (akua) or mere men. A major revelation to these first Hawaiians aboard was the rife presence of metal objects on the ship. Metal was only known to the Hawaiians from legends and from objects found washed onto their beaches from wrecked Asian or European ships, the most prominent example being a samurai sword that entered into their lore in the sixteenth century and was eventually passed into the successive possession of Kaua'i's rulers after the powerful King Kukona.[22]

---

[21] Kamakau 1992, p. 92.

[22] Kalakaua, 1990, pp. 175-205 and, without mention of the sword, the section "Kukona" in Wichman, 2003, pp. 47-52, also see Chapman 2004, p. 60.

The next group of Hawaiians to come aboard Captain Cook's *Resolution* included a warrior of Ka'eo's guard named Kapupu'u, who disregarded the advice of the previously visiting kahuna Kū'ohu that he was "not to meddle with the things belonging to the Gods" and seized a number of iron objects, placed them in his canoe, and attempted to paddle away. One of the British sailors fired his musket and killed Kapupu'u, who thus became the first casualty of the intercultural meeting. The Hawai'ians were shocked to see him slain by a British firearm. They thought the expelled rush of smoke was water, and called the "Gods'" weapon, beyond their ken, as a "wai-ki'" (water squirter) or "wai-pahu" (booming water gusher).

When Captain Cook and his men came ashore to the village of Waimea looking to replenish the ships' supply of fresh water, they encountered Ka'eo and Kamakahelei directly, Ka'eo wearing a resplendant feather "mahiole" cap and "'ahu-'ula" cape. According to Kamakau, some of their chiefs cried "Let's kill these people for killing Kapupu'u." But kahuna Kū'ohu spoke up forcefully, saying "that is not a good thought, for they were not to blame. The fault was ours for plundering, for Kapupu'u went to plunder. I have told you that we live under a law; if any man rob or steal, his bones will be stripped of flesh. The proper way to do is to treat these people kindly." Kū'ohu also admitted that he "did not know whether these are gods or men. But he went on metaphorically to say "here is the test of a god: if we tempt them and

1775 portrait of Captain James Cook (7 November, 1728-14 February, 1779) by Nathaniel Dance-Holland (1735-1811) from: http://en.wikipedia.org/wiki/James_Cook.

they do not open their gourd container which holds their ancestral gods (' 'aumakua') then they are themselves gods, but if they open the sacred gourds ('ipu kapu') [that is, if they yield to the temptation of women], then they are not gods—they are foreigners."

When Captain Cook and his men were preparing to return to their ships, Ka'eo and Kamakahelei had them presented with gifts from Kaua'i's natural bounty—hogs, chickens, bananas, taro, potatoes, sugar cane, yams, fine woven mats, and bark cloth. In exchange Captain Cook gave to the Hawaiians gifts of cloth, iron, knives, necklaces, and hand-held mirrors. But, according to Kamakau, Ka'eo was also interested to see how Captain Cook would react to kahuna Kū'ohu's "temptation test."[23] He gave Kamakahelei's daughter with Kina, Lelemahoalani, to Captain Cook, making clear that she might be used for his sexual pleasure. Captain Cook then gave Ka'eo further gifts, including a sword. Kamakau then states that "when the other women noticed that the chiefess had slept with foreigners, they too slept with foreigners in order to obtain cloth, iron, and mirrors."

After this relation, Kamakau, writing in the mid nineteenth century, writes that "to these islands, he (Captain Cook) bequeathed such possessions as the

---

[23] Kamakau 1992, p. 95.

flea, never known on them before this day, and prostitution, with its results, syphilis and other venereal diseases," which "caused the dwindling of the population after the coming of Captain Cook."[24]

As for Captain Cook's personal participation, as opposed to the clear contributions of his crew, in the spreading of venereal diseases among the Hawaiians, historians are unsure. Kamakau does not directly state that Cook had sexual relations with Lelemahoalani…but he apparently does believe it and does imply it in the relation cited here. We can read from Captain Cook's memoirs his own awareness that his sailors did indeed spread venereal disease among the natives they visited. The pay book of the *Resolution* showed that 66 men of the total crew of 112 had venereal diseases.[25] The spread in Hawaii was so rapid that he observed visible venereal lesions and rashes among natives on other of the Hawaiian islands only a year after his first visit to Kaua'i (he died in a skirmish with King Kalaniopu'u's warriors at Kealakekua Bay on Hawai'i island on February 14, 1779). As for her sexual relations with the foreigners, Kamakau repeats a report from "one man"

---

[24] Ibid, pp. 95-96, and see also Captain George Vancouver's 1792 impression, as reported in Ridley 2010, pp. 258-9.

[25] Joesting 1984, p. 39.

who "said the woman [Lelemahoalani] who was on the ship says that they (the foreigners) groan when they are hurt. When the woman sticks her nails into them, they say, "You scratch like an owl; your nails are too long; you claw like a duck!"[26]

Unfinished 1795 painting by Johann Zoffany (1733-1818) of "The Death of Captain James Cook, 14 February, 1779" at Kealakekua Bay on the big island of Hawai'i's west coast. From: http://en.wikipedia.org/wiki/James_Cook.

---

[26] Ibid, p. 101.

Hawaiian historian John F. G. Stokes, in his "Origin of the Condemnation of Captain Cook in Hawaii"[27] refutes Kamakau's relation of Cook's exchanging gifts for sexual relations with Lelemahoalani. Still other sources, both native and foreign, say that Captain Cook impregnated Kamakahelei herself when she offered him her own "temptation test," and that this pregnancy resulted in King Kaumuali'i's birth, thus accounting for Kaumuali'i's "nose and general features like a white man's."[28] Cook's ship's surgeon William Ellis wrote in his memoirs of the meeting that chiefess Kamakahelei was "short and lusty...and very plain with respect to person," the implication, perhaps, being that Captain Cook would not have found her attractive. Yet another rumor, recounted in Wichman is that Kaumuali'i is the biological child of Captain Cook and his own half sister Lelemahoalani.[29] Obviously those who credit these rumors of Captain Cook's paternity of Kaumuali'i will, counter to considerable evidence to the contrary, list Kaumuali'i's birth year as 1778 instead of 1780 as in Wichman and here.[30]

---

[27] Stokes 1930, pp. 68-111.

[28] Kamakau 1992, p.254.

[29] Wichman 2003, p. 145.

[30] Zambucka 1999, p. 2.

THE RAISING OF KAUMUALI'I:

It was the Hawaiian custom, called "hānai," of the high ali'i to have those of their children who were intended future rulers adopted by others of their relatives to raise through their dependent childhood. In this way Kamakahelei's son with Kaneoneo, Keawe, who was born about 1777, was given in a hānai arrangement to the family of Wailua District senior Chieftain Inamo'o. (Wailua is on the eastern side of Kaua'i). The younger son, Kaumuali'i, from husband Ka'eo, was not adopted out to others to raise, because when he was born he was not the presumed heir and successor. His older half-brother Keawe was. So Kaumuali'i, despite his being the son of Ka'eo, whose ancestral mana was generally considered even more powerful than that of Keawe's father, Kaneoneo, was instead raised in the Wailua household of his mother…and this fact had significance to the development of his character. His mother was the primary influence in his young life, since his father Ka'eo was often away on military campaigns on the other islands.

Keawe grew up in the Wailua family compound of Chief Inamo'o thinking that he would one day become the Ali'i nui of Kaua'i, Ni'ihau, and Lehua. His mother, Kamakahelei, had complicated this succession by marrying, in 1777, Kaumuali'i's father Ka'eo eight years before Keawe's father Kaneoneo died…this is because, unlike the commoners, the Hawaiian ali'i were polygamous. Kaneoneo fought in an unsuccessful rebellion (the "Waipi'o kimopo") of the O'ahu chiefs against the Maui rule of Ka'eo's half-brother Kahekili in 1785. He died in fierce combat at Kalamake'e.[31] The legendarily ferocious Kahekili, the right half of his body tattooed black from head to foot in honor of the thunder God Kāne-Hekili,[32] ordered the mutilation of the bodies of all the slain O'ahu chiefesses who possessed, as Kaneoneo did, the "kapu moe" (prostrating taboo). The rebel chiefs who were captured were placed while still alive into the great oven of Kuna in Waikiki. Kahekili then built the frame of a "hale" (grass-thatched house) with his victims' bones.[33]

Keawe's younger half-brother Kaumuali'i also thought that he would one day become the Ali'i

---

[31] Kamakau 1992 p. 140.

[32] See "Tattoos" in Bibliography for evidence of right side.

[33] See mention of a "pā'iwi kanaka" (fence made of human bones) in Ho'omanawanui 2012, p. 215. See also Daws 1974, p. 31.

nui of Kaua'i, Ni'ihau, and Lehua. His father Ka'eo told him that this would be assured by his "more powerful mana." But Kaumuali'i's mother Kamakaheilei (who had herself been named Kaua'i's ruling ali'i by her grandfather Peleiōhōlani in lieu of her lesser-mana father and Peleiōhōlani's son-in-law Kaumehe'iwā after the death of her mother, Peleiōhōlani's daughter, Ka'apuwai) would not relinquish his care to any of the chiefs as she had with Keawe, and so the matter of succession was not clear. Kaumuali'i and his older half-brother Keawe were therefore "mana rivals."

It was, then, Kamakahelei who personally taught Kaumuali'i to chant his very long "mele inoa," or "song of identity," reciting his personal genealogical connection through the past kings back to the Hawaiian gods and thus evidencing his powerful mana. Indeed the ability to chant this connection to the gods ("akua") was essential to a person's status as an ali'i. It was forbidden ("kapu") for commoners ("maka'ainana") even to mention their forebears in chants...and punishable by death.[34] Only the ali'i were able to connect themselves to the gods by means of these chants. And memorizing and reciting such long chants with the required exactitude was very difficult and

---

[34] Kirch 2012, p. 219.

took most of the ruling ali'i years of their childhood to accomplish.

We know that young Kaumuali'i had to include in his name chant his own 22 ruling predecessors as the independent King ("Ali'i Aimoku") of Kaua'i. Kamakau[35], Wichman, Buyers, and Wikipedia (entry on "Alii Aimoku of Kauai") agree that these are: 1) Moikewa (ca. 1280 AD according to Wichman's estimate), 2) Haulanuiaiakea, 3) La'amaikahiki, 4) Ahukini-a-la'a, 5) Kamahano, 6) Luanu'u, 7) Kukona, 8) Manokalanipo, 9) Kamakamano, 10) Kahakuakane, 11) Kuwaiupaukamoku, 12) Kahakumakapaweo, 13) Kalanikukuma, 14) Kahakumakalina, 15) Kamakapu, 16) Kawelomahamahaia, 17) Kawelomakualua, 18) Kaweloaikanaka, 19) Kaweloamaihunali'i, 20) Kuali'i (also 19th Ali'i Amoku of O'ahu), 21) Peleioholani (1730-1770 AD, also 22nd Alii Aimoku of O'ahu), and 22) Kamakahelei (female, born ca. 1750, ruled 1770-1794, Kaumuali'i's mother). But this is only a fraction of Kaumuali'i's entire name chant. In "Hawaiian Antiquities,[36]" David Malo lists 59 kings of the Hawai'i island line between the god-person and sky-father Wakea, whose wife was earth-mother Papa...the first people in the Hawaiian (as opposed to Polynesian) origins mythology,

---

[35] Kamakau1992, p. 448.

[36] Malo 1997, p. 238.

and fifteenth-century Hawai'i island King Liloa, an important predecessor in Kamehameha's line.

It's difficult for us to imagine such a feat of memorization as was required of these rulers and their priests...essentially the islands' oral historians.[37] But despite the difficulty, young Kaumuali'i took joy in the task of learning and mastered his chant in such a short time that his parents' priests ("kahuna") were positively impressed and came to respect his prodigious memory and quick mind.[38] These priests explained to Kaumuali'i the need to respect and enforce the Hawaiian system of "kapus" and also the sacrifices (including human sacrifices) which pleased the gods so that they protected the people of Kaua'i from natural disasters, from privation, and from subjugation by other peoples. As a result of this instruction, Kaumuali'i became quite religious even as a youth and spent significant time in prayer ("pule"), seeking advice from the gods.

In his youth, Kaumuali'i learned to fish with hooks and spears and nets. He learned to manage fish in manmade ponds. He learned to plant and harvest the taro in irrigated plots called "lo'i." Because all meal preparation was the duty of men, he

---

[37] See Kāne 1997, p. 39.

[38] See the encomium in Warne 2008, p. 21, and see nupepa.org for "He Mele no Kaumuali'i."

learned to pound the taro corms into poi, though, as a high ali'i, he would never be required to do it. He learned how clothing and canoes were made. He grew up to be tall and strong like his father, and in his teens established himself as one of Kaua'i's foremost aquatic athletes. He could stay under water longer, swim faster, and surf the waves more ably than anyone else.[39] He could paddle canoes more strongly than others of his cohort for hours and hours without resting. He made "spirit leaps" into the water from many of Kaua'i's prominent heights to "prove his mana."[40] And he became proficient in the use of weapons... wooden daggers and spears, shark-toothed clubs, and, in his early adulthood, western metal swords, firearms and cannon.

    Kamakahelei liked to travel around to the villages of Kaua'i that were dedicated to particular purposes. She would show Kaumuali'i where, in the valley above Waimea and in the forested highlands of Koke'e were the villages that specialized in producing canoes and paddles of such strength and quality that they were sought by the rulers of the other islands. The high forest there also hosted a "hale-manu" (bird haven) where colorful feathers were gathered. On the way back overland by bearer-borne litter ("mānele"), she would take Kau-

---

[39] Ellis 2004, p. 377.

[40] Dickey 2014, p. 28, and Wichman 1998, p. 11)

muali'i to the salt ponds near Hanapēpē where the best salt was produced by evaporation of sea water on carefully groomed pond lots. The mildly intoxicating drink called " 'awa" was made near Koloa by villagers, young women mostly, who would spit the chewed stems and roots of the pepper plant (*Piper methysticum)* into calabash containers, then dilute the saliva-softened expectorate into this ceremonial drink favored by the ali'i.[41] On the north shore of Kaua'i was a village near Ha'ena where Chiefess Kekela, a refugee from the O'ahu rebellion that cost Kamakahelei's husband Kaneoneo his life, showed Kamakahelei her people who collected wild bird feathers: black and yellow feathers from the "ō-ō" and the "mamo," red feathers from the "i'iwi" and the "apapane." The birds were captured alive on gummed branches or with nets and only those with but a few feathers to pluck (o-o and mamo) could be released. Any of the villagers, women and children too, might take part in the collection of the feathers, but here the ali'i "'ahu'ula" capes and "mahiole" caps were made by meticulous male craftsmen by attaching each feather bundle to a netting made from very strong olona

---

[41] See descriptions of the drink's negative effects (scrofula, eczema) on Ka'eo and Inamo'o in Ridley 2010, p. 296, 299.

fiber.[42] Each cape contained many thousands of feathers and the production of a single cape took as long as a year.

THE ANE'EKAPUAHI: PRAYING A PERSON TO DEATH:

Kaumuali'i's mother, Kamakahelei, encouraged the religious aspect of his character and taught him a prayer she had no doubt learned from the kahuna lineage of the sorcery goddess Kapo (a younger sister of Pele, the goddess of volcanoes and fire). The prayer, one of the "pule'ana'ana" (death prayers) was called the "ane'ekapuahi," and it took three days to prepare and complete.[43] The purpose of the ane'ekapuahi was to request Kapo to cause the incineration of the person named in the prayer. After Kaumuali'i's mastery of the ane'ekapuahi became known in his adulthood, he was feared as a man who could "pray a person to a fiery death."[44]

---

[42] See Kaeppler, Linnekin 1990, pp. 47-55 for "Who Made the Feather Cloaks?," also Wikipedia under "'ahu'ula," and for a "how to" see Te Rangi Hiroa (Buck), pp. 231-248.

[43] Zambucka 1999, p. 12, Kamakau 1992, p. 194.

[44] Gutmanis 1983, p. 27.

KAUMUALI'I VALUES EDUCATION, LEARNS ENGLISH:

Kaumuali'i as a young man was always curious, asking frequent questions of his elders and of the foreign seafarers who followed the example of Britain's Captain James Cook to find their way to the Hawaiian Islands. These foreigners became very important in Kaumuali'i's life. The first very impactful such foreigner was English Captain George Vancouver, whom he first met in 1792 when he was twelve years old.[45] He applied himself especially enthusiastically to the study of Vancouver's "foreign language"--English. In time his skill in English became immensely valuable to him, as he used it to communicate with diverse English and American seamen, traders, and, later, missionaries. Helping him in this effort from his impressionable early teens were three sailors named John Rowbottom, John Williams, and James Coleman.[46] These three hardies were left

---

[45] Earlier contact with foreign captains include James Colnett and Manuel Quimper, a Spanish Captain who observed young Kaumuali'i being "carried in a reclining position as an indication of his status." See Mills 2002, p.74.

[46] See Ridley 2010, pp. 259-262, and Wichman 1998, p. 11-12. Also an earlier "beachcomber" named Samuel Hitchcock, a favorite of Ka'eo's since 1788…see Mills 2002, p. 75.

An 18th century portrait believed to be that of Capt. George Vancouver (June 22, 1757-May 10, 1798). From Wikipedia.

behind on Kaua'i to collect aromatic "'iliahi" (sandalwood) by American Captain John Kendrick of the *Lady Washington* in 1793. They gave Kaumuali'i much of his first English language instruction, albeit of a very rough, often profane, quality. Young Kaumuali'i spent as much time as he could in their adventurous company. Later Kaumuali'i engaged Boston seaman John Gowan as his interpreter and instructor of English. It was Gowan who pointed out to Kaumuali'i that there were different levels of English that he should speak to different people in different circumstances...and this Kaumuali'i learned to do. His conversational English became quite facile and he learned to read and write some as well. He learned western weights and measures, months, years, and seasons…all kinds of tools and implements. His command of English and its host cultures' history and politics impressed visitor after visitor. He soon came to call himself in English by the name "George," at the suggestion of Captain George Vancouver, after the English King George III, as well as the American President George Washington. He later also gave his son, Humehume, the English name "George," and, after this son's eventual return to Kaua'i, wrote an English letter to thank the American Board of Commissioners for Foreign Missions for helping his son.[47]

KAUMUALI'I'S MARRIAGES AND CHILDREN:

When Kaumuali'i was thirteen years old, Kamakahelei talked with him about his need to "marry well" in the "pi'o" or "ni'aupi'o" way. The Hawaiian ali'i, in order not to dilute and thus diminish their "mana," practiced not only polygamy, marrying more than one spouse, but they also married and had children with genetic relatives, the closer the better, in order to result in the purest possible genealogical connection to their gods. Marriage and reproduction by full siblings or, even more desirably twins, was the optimal "ni'aupi'o"

---

[47] Warne 2008, p. 141.

marriage in their consideration, the best possible for an ali'i nui.⁴⁸ That is why, Kamakahelei told Kaumuali'i, that he should, when he was ready, marry his older half-sisters by Kaneoneo— Kapua'amohu, Kapiolani, or Kaininoa (Naoa) in preference to his less desirable by mana even older half-sisters by Kina— Lelemahoalani, Kawalu or Kaluaipihana…and that he should certainly confine his marriages only to high-ranking ali'i wives. He might, she suggested, exempt Lelemahoalani as a marital candidate because she was already "well married" to an ali'i chief. But in no circumstance should he marry a "maka'āinana" (commoner) woman. The child of such a marriage could not succeed to rule Kaua'i or any other Hawaiian island. He could engage in intimate relations with whomever he may desire…ali'i or commoner…but his marriages had to be carefully considered in this "pi'o" way.

When foreigners asked Kaumuali'i in his later adulthood how many wives he had, he gave only the answer, "Many." Scholars know the names of nine or ten.⁴⁹ In order from approximately 1796 they are: Kapua'amohu (m. ca. 1796), Namahana

---

⁴⁸ On this and the genealogical classes of ali'i, kapus, enforcement, and exemptions…see Kamakau 1964 on "Society," pp. 3-22.

⁴⁹ Croft 2012B, p. 359 with addition of Dean Kekoolani's genealogy.

(m. ca. 1798), Kawalu (m. 1799), Kaininoa (Naoa) (m. 1801), Monalau (m. ca. 1802), Naluahi (m. ca. 1803), Makua (m. ca. 1806), Kekaiha'akulou (later Deborah Kapule, m. 1809)), and (by abduction) Hawaiian Regent Ka'ahumanu (m. 1821). More than once, Kaumuali'i sent chiefs as emissaries to Tahiti to bring him back prospective ali'i wives, but these efforts failed.[50] We do not know for sure who was the mother of his oldest son Humehume,[51] whom he paid a great sum to send for his education to America at the age of four with Captain James Rowan of the Boston ship *Hazard* in early 1804, but she was described as a "maka'āinana," or "commoner," making Humehume traditionally ineligible to be Kaumuali'i's legitimate heir and successor. Kaumuali'i's legitimate heir and intended successor was his son with first wife and queen Kapua'amohu, who was also Kaumuali'i's older half-sister and the full sister of his rival Keawe. This son was Keali'iahonui, born August 17th of 1800, who grew to nearly seven feet of height by his middle teens and had a remarkable singing voice. In addition to sons Humehume and Keali'iahonui, Kaumuali'i had a younger son from Namahana, born about 1806 named Kahekili after the great Mau'i federation king, and three daughters: Kekaulike Kinoiki, from Kapua'amohu, Kapiolani from Naoa, and Nahinu

---

[50] Zambucka 1999, p. 20.

[51] See Kekoolani site to find "Ni'ihau."

from Naluahi.⁵² With non-married commoners or even ali'i others he had other children.⁵³ We don't know how many and we don't know many names. Some of Kaumuali'i's issue is involved in modern claims of Hawaiian royalty.⁵⁴ Once he told Dr. George Anton Schaeffer that "one of his wives went away with his interpreter John Gowan." Which wife is not entirely certain, but I figure by exclusion of later mentioned others that Makua is the most likely candidate.

KAUMUALI'I'S RIVALRY WITH KEAWE— THE PROMISE:

When Kaumuali'i asked his mother Kamakahelei about whether he or his older half-brother Keawe would become the ali'i nui of Kaua'i, she told him non-commitally that both he and Keawe were possible successors to rule. "But," she told him, "you must promise me that you will never raise your hand against your brother. And I have made Keawe

---

⁵² See Kekoolani's genealogy, and Joesting 1987, p. 11.

⁵³ See Fujimoto 2014 for evidence of a male child named Kainoahou, meaning "the sea is free," from the family of a current Waimea resident that I know.

⁵⁴ Croft 2012B, p. 360, and see Silva.

promise also that he will never raise his hand against you." Then she asked him, "Do you

The modern statue of Kamakahelei, depicted late in her life by Karen Lucas, at the Chiefess Kamakahelei Middle School, 4431 Nuhou Street, Lihue, HI 96766. See http://ckms.k12.hi.us. Photograph by Lee B. Croft, June 2014.

promise?" And when he answered " 'ae" (yes), she said seriously, "I will inform the priests."

In conversations with several foreign visitors, Kaumuali'i spoke of his mother Kamakahelei's preference for peace instead of war, and even of her personal opposition to some of his father Ka'eo's aggressive ideas. "She believed in Aloha," he told them. "She would tell me about how the rulers and chiefs of the other islands would kill their subjects without mercy for no good reason… women and children slaughtered just for fish bait."[55] "I don't want my people to remember me that way," she would say. "In all your dealing with people…ali'i or commoners alike…or with foreigners too…be fair, be kind… 'malama pono' ('preserve justice and right')…practice Aloha. That's what I desire from you, my son." When his mother's name was mentioned, Kaumuali'i would say: "E ola hau ka inoa 'o Kamakahelei" (Let the name of Kamakahelei live on).

KAUMUALI'I'S PARENTS GO TO WAR ON O'AHU:

When Kaumuali'i was fourteen years old in late 1794, his mother went to join his father, Ka'eo,

---

[55] People as fish bait, Kamakau 1992, p. 171, Mills 2002, p. 75, and Pierce 1976, p. 181.

and a large contingent of Kaua'i's warriors who were campaigning on adjacent O'ahu to take control of the island from Ka'eo's nephew, Chief Kalanikūpule, after the death at Waikīkī of Maui federation king Kahekili. At first, Ka'eo's troops dominated the O'ahu forces, but at the Battle of Kalau'ao in December of that year Kalanikūpule gained the aid of three western ships by promising a great number of O'ahu hogs to one of the Captains, British whaler William Brown, who had charge of both the *Jackal* and the smaller *Prince Lee Boo*.[56] Captain Brown had an Italian mercenary sharpshooter and cannoneer the Hawaiians called Mare Amara aboard advising his crew in the conflict, and Amara, who had previously fought on the side of Ka'eo and therefore knew him, directed the ship's cannon fire with such accuracy that Kaumuali'i's parents, Ka'eo and Kamakahelei, were both found and killed by Kalanikūpule's warriors.[57] I suppose that Ka'eo's trained fighting dogs were also killed. As a result of this, O'ahu Chief Kalanikūpule's forces prevailed in the battle and cannoneer Mare Amara was likely given Ka'eo's brightly feathered mahiole cap and 'ahu'ula cape as a prize.

---

[56] Massey 2009, p. 97, and be sure to watch the superb "composited" accompanying DVD.

[57] See Daws 1974, p. 39, and Ridley 2010, pp. 347-352.

INAMO'O BECOMES REGENT:

When he heard the news of both his parents' death from the surviving Kaua'i mū and warrior, Ki'ikīkī, Kaumuali'i was grief-stricken and angry. Both he and his half-brother Keawe were considered too young to rule, so the aged Wailua chieftain Inamo'o took over as the regent of Kaua'i and Ni'ihau in Keawe's stead, by-passing the younger Kaumuali'i, who by then was known to be Ka'eo's designated successor.

KAUMUALI'I'S ANE'EKAPUAHI REVENGE:

The next month Captain Brown and his crew were working ashore to refit and rerig the ship *Jackal* near Pearl Harbor on O'ahu. Kalanikūpule and his war chieftain Komohomoho devised a plan to take over both the *Jackal* and the *Prince Lee Boo* during the slaughtering and salting of the promised hogs. The O'ahu warriors suddenly attacked the ships' company, killing Captain Brown and most of the two ships' officers. Kalanikūpule then took possession of both of Captain Brown's ships. Kalanikūpule spared cannoneer Mare Amara, who agreed to help him, but imprisoned the remaining members of the crews below their ships' decks and set sail from Honolulu in command of the two ships for Hawai'i Island.

O'ahu chief Kalanikūpule's intention was to use the ships' cannons and munitions to attack Kamehameha, the King of the big island of Hawai'i, and put an early end to Kamehameha's long campaign to extend his rule throughout all the main inhabited Hawaiian islands. But a strange sudden seasickness enveloped the O'ahu warriors on the larger ship *Jackal* so that the imprisoned crew members, in a quite heroic hand-to-hand struggle against a greater number of sickened warriors, won back their ships. They put Kalanikūpule, his queen, three women of his entourage, and a servant under guard and cleared the ships of all the warriors, throwing them off the deck to swim ashore onto Waikīkī Beach.

Under the command of seamen George Lamport (on the *Jackal*) and William Bonallack (on the *Prince Lee Boo),* they decided to sail to Hawai'i Island anyway, but to contribute their aid to Kamehameha's campaign instead of attacking him. This historic move proved to be of great benefit to Kamehameha in his campaign to conquer all the other islands. They right away made Kalanikūpule and his party witness the execution of Mare Amara, whom they then considered a turncoat, by burning him alive on the deck of the *Jackal* in a pan of his own gunpowder. Then, off Diamond Head, they set Kalanikūpule, his queen, and his servant in a captured canoe and let them paddle away. They took the three consort women with them to Hawai'i.

When he heard about these events, Kaumuali'i considered Amara's fiery demise the consequence of his ane'ekapuahi prayer...that it was the sorcery goddess Kapo, at his prayer's request, who had caused Amara's incineration and granted him revenge for the deaths of his parents.[58] There is evidence that even Kamehameha interpreted this event in this way, so that he was ever after uncharacteristically cautious in his dealings with Kaumuali'i.

FIRST MARRIAGE—KAPUA'AMOHU:

During the Kaua'i regency of Inamo'o in 1796, Kaumuali'i, age 16, married his older half-sister by Kaneoneo, his rival Keawe's full sister, Kapua'amohu, thus strategically removing her as a candidate for a more powerful "ni'aupi'o" marriage to Keawe. Kapua'amohu then moved into her own personal hale in the royal compound in Wailua as a kind of "queen in waiting" for Kaumuali'i.

---

[58] Croft 2012B, pp. 245-248, Massey, pp. 107-110.

KING KAMEHAMEHA TAKES O'AHU— THE BATTLE OF NU'UANU:

The great king Kamehameha of the big island of Hawai'i had won an important victory in an amphibious invasion of O'ahu in April of the previous year, 1795. At the decisive Battle of Nu'uanu, in which as many as 25,000 warriors took part...the largest battle on what would become U.S. territory until the Civil War Battle of Gettysburg[59]...the last remnants of Chief Kalanikūpule's forces were pushed off a 400-foot cliff ("pali") into the howling wind like "kaleleka'ani" ("leaping fish"). The painting of this action displayed at the Overlook site at the summit of O'ahu's Pali highway by "Living Treasure of Hawaii" artist Herb Kawainui Kāne (1928-2011) is a stunning testament to the ferocity of this historic battle.

KEKUPUOHI AND THE DEATH OF KA'IANA:

Earlier in the battle, at La'imi, the high ali'i Ka'iana 'Ahu'ula, an influential prince of Kaua'i (Ka'eo's hated first cousin) in Kaumuali'i's childhood years, who had been taken to China, the Philippines, and America by British Captain John

---

[59] Dukas 2010, p. vii.

Meares on the *Nootka* in 1787, had been killed by Kamehameha's forces. After "seeing the world" with Captain Meares, Ka'iana had returned to Hawai'i island experienced in English and in the use of western weaponry to become a high chief for King Kamehameha. He is also reputed to have become romantically involved there with Kamehameha's favorite wife Ka'ahumanu, causing Kamehameha to place a kapu on Ka'ahumanu for him in particular, since he was apparently undeterred by Ka'ahumanu's "hump-backed boy" chastity monitor.[60]

Ka'iana had led some of Kamehameha's forces to O'ahu, but then, fearing that Kamehameha's jealous chiefs planned to kill him, switched his loyalty to lead some of Kalanikūpule's forces just before the Battle of Nu'uanu. Historical sources differ on just how he was killed. Was he speared by Kamehameha's warriors,[61] hit by stone shrapnel from a cannon ball fired by Kamehameha's English advisor John Young,[62] killed by multiple musket shots,[63] or was he clubbed on the head and

---

[60] Silverman 1987, p. 20, Croft 2012B, p. 148.

[61] Cahill 1999, p. 83.

[62] Mitchell 1992, p. 289.

[63] B.K. Parker's 2016 blog entry, citing Desha.

killed by a priest?⁶⁴ But these sources agree that Ka'iana's wife Kekupuohi, who had chosen to

This lithograph by Spoilum (Guan Zuolin…see https://en.wikipedia.org/wiki/spoilum) is entitled "Tianna, a Prince of Atooi" ("Ka'iana, a Prince of Kaua'i") from Captain John Meares's Voyages Made in the Years 1788 and 1789, from Wikipedia. Notice his 'ahu'ula cape and mahiole cap.

---

⁶⁴ Miller 1988, p. 15.

remain loyal to Kamehameha and even fight on his side, nevertheless made her way to Ka'iana amidst the battle to comfort him as he lay dying.[65] "It is said that the shooting on both sides stopped as both enemies and friends shed tears of sadness. Kekupuohi then chanted a beautiful farewell oli (chant)."[66] A heiau (holy place) was built at his death site, now on the grounds of the Mauna Ala resting place of the ali'i in Honolulu.[67]

THE VANQUISHED ARE SACRIFICED, WESTERN ADVISORS SPARED:

Kalanikūpule, though wounded, escaped the final slaughter of his warriors at the Nu'uanu pali with his high chiefs and three foreign advisors: Australians "Miller" and "Black Jack," (who later designed a two-story house for Ka'ahumanu in Lahaina, Maui) and Massachusetts native Oliver Holmes (later O'ahu governor for Kamehameha).

---

[65] See Dukas 2010, pp. 44-45.

[66] See Parker's website, pp. 4.

[67] Miller 1988, pp. 1-19, and see relation "The Story of Ka'iana" by Mel Kalahiki at http://pacificworlds.com and "Ka'iana and Kekupuohi" by Brook Kapūkuniahi Parker at http://hawaiianatart.com .

But the fugitive Kalanikūpule was killed months later in 'Ewa and his chiefs and advisors captured. Kalanikūpule's body was sacrificed at a Moanalua Valley heiau with one of his thigh bones used by Kamehameha in a kāhili's shaft (a feather standard signifying royalty). This kāhili is now in the Bishop Museum.[68] Kamehameha gave prominent positions in his entourage to Miller ("Mela"), Black Jack ("Keaka 'ele'ele"), and Holmes ("Homa"), but ordered the captured chiefs stuffed alive into the Kuna oven in Waikīkī...something Holmes later told Dr. George Anton Schaeffer "is a very hard thing to forget."[69] Only did Kalanikupule's brother Kaolaulani escape being sacrificed by canoeing to Kaua'i and gaining sanctuary there from regent Inamo'o.

KAMEHAMEHA'S 1796 ATTEMPT TO TAKE KAUA'I:

On the strength of his impressive victory over Kalanikūpule, Kamehameha added O'ahu to his control of the islands of Hawai'i, Maui, Kaho'olawe, Lana'i, and Moloka'i. The only inhabited Hawaiian Islands left out of his control were now Kaua'i, Ni'ihau, and tiny Lehua, which were ruled

---

[68] Chapman 2004, p. 17.

[69] Croft 2012B, pp. 167-173.

by an aged regent in the stead of one of two juveniles, Keawe or Kaumuali'i. So, Kamehameha mounted a large-scale attack to achieve his final goal, control of the kingdom of Kaua'i. The fleet Kamehameha had constructed of 1,500 canoes, carrying 10,000 warriors, many of whom were armed with western muskets, far surpassed any defensive force the Kaua'i regent Inamo'o could muster. But strong winds came up in the seventy-mile Ka'ie'ie Waho Channel between O'ahu and Kaua'i, sinking many boats and scattering others, so that Kamehameha was forced to give the order for his fleet to return to O'ahu. Some of the warriors, however, could not hear this command while struggling with the surging sea and the whistling wind. About a thousand of them persevered to land on Kaua'i's southeastern beaches (now Shipwreck and Maha'ulepu), where Inamo'o's defensive forces, now numerically superior and more familiar with the territory, slaughtered them almost entirely and captured their canoes. Legends say that only three men survived to reach a sanctuary (Piha Ke'kua, now developed as the "Po'ipu Crater"?) from which they eventually returned to O'ahu to tell Kamehameha of his men's grim fate. But Kamehameha had by that time abandoned the effort in order to quell a rebellion on his home island of Hawai'i led by chief Namakeha, the "sun shunner," who was a brother of Ka'iana.[70] It was

---

[70] Kamakau 1992, pp. 173-174.

in Kaua'i's struggle between Kamehameha's exhausted seaborne warriors and Kauai's home guards directed by the regent Inamo'o that the rival young half-brothers, Keawe and Kaumuali'i, witnessed combat deaths for the first time. And, the exertion of the effort was apparently too much for the old Inamo'o, who died soon afterwards.[71]

BROTHER KEAWE TAKES COMMAND:

Upon regent Inamo'o's death, Keawe quickly claimed the position of "ali'i nui" of Kaua'i, Ni'ihau and Lehua. With a contingent of warriors he took his younger half-brother Kaumuali'i captive in a skirmish in Wailua, and assigned the royal "mū" bodyguards to keep Kaumuali'i, of whom he was quite jealous, under a kind of "house arrest" in the Wailua compound. He quickly took command of Inamo'o's stock of foreign firearms to help enforce his rule, keeping them hidden under the watch of his mū.

Kaumuali'i's monitoring guards included Ki'ikīkī, one of the first three men to board Captain Cook's *Resolution* in 1778 who had served as Ka'eo's second-in-command in the battles on O'ahu in 1785 and, treacherously, in the 1794 defeat on O'ahu. Ki'ikīkī had been born in Kaua'i's

---

[71] See Ridley 2010, pp. 298-9.

northern ahupua'a (prefecture) of Wainiha, famous for its history of contributing mū to the ali'i of Kaua'i and even other islands. He had become the "konohiki" (tax collector chief) of Wainiha. He was renowned for his physical strength. He could, it was said, "pull trees out of the ground" and pick up and throw "pig-sized boulders" at his enemies. He spent much time in his youth practicing the Hawaiian martial art called "lua" (greatly skilled fighting, largely by hand), which in one of its moves depended upon the strength to lift opponents over the head and drop them forcefully onto one's knees, breaking their bones. In addition to Ki'ikīkī, Kaumuali'i was also guarded by Ki'ikīkī's older brother Kāne'eku, who was konohiki of Hanapēpē. But it was only Ki'ikīkī who kept possession of the firearms taken from the deceased Inamo'o's cache.

THE MANA LEAP FROM WAILUA FALLS:

During one of his visits to his half-brother, Keawe told Kaumuali'i that he, Keawe, had made a powerful "mana leap" from the top of Wailua Falls (called then "Wai'ehu") and that his success in surviving such a tall leap meant that his mana was stronger than Kaumuali'i's. "The gods want me to rule," Keawe said. This caused Kaumuali'i to request permission from his guard Ki'ikīkī to be

Kaumuali'i's "mana leap" from the top of Wailua Falls by **Brook Kapūkuniahi Parker**, 2012.

accompanied out of the Wailua royal compound to the nearby Wailua Falls so that he could make such a mana leap himself. Ki'ikīkī assented to this. He accompanied Kaumuali'i to the falls and witnessed him leap from the top into the water more than a hundred feet below. Ki'ikīkī then told Kaumuali'i that Keawe had lied to him about surviving the leap himself. Keawe had, Ki'ikīkī said, gone to the top of the falls in his company, but that his thoughts had been seized by cowardice when he looked down, and he could not make the leap. He had told Kaumuali'i that he had made the leap and survived it just to entice Kaumuali'i into making the leap himself and dying in the attempt. Tricking him into making the leap, Ki'ikīkī said, was Keawe's way of murdering him.[72]

Kaumuali'i was very angry with Keawe for lying to him about his mana leap from the top of Wailua Falls. His own survival in making the leap gave him confidence that the gods wanted him, and not Keawe, to be the ali'i nui.[73] But Keawe had him confined and closely watched every day and Kaumuali'i had no immediately apparent way to get the better of Keawe. To him, it appeared that Keawe would very soon find another way, without personally "raising his hand" against him, to have him killed.

KAPUA'AMOHU'S CHOICE:

Stories of how Kaumuali'i gained control of the firearms and then had Keawe killed with one of them involve his older half-sister wife Kapua'amohu, who was put into a difficult position

---

[72] See note with "Wailua Falls" in the Biblio. to see a modern jump.

[73] Dickey 2014, p. 28, Wichman 1998, p. 11.

indeed.[74] She had to decide whether she would side with her half-brother husband or her closer-in-age full brother in their life-or-death struggle with each other. She knew that she would be the wife and queen of whomever of them managed to have the other eliminated. Her choice to support her husband Kaumuali'i had historic consequences for Kaua'i, especially since Keawe had told others that he planned to join forces with Kamehameha.[75]

The stories say that, using the sexual favors of Kapua'amohu as a bribe, Kaumuali'i persuaded Ki'ikīkī's friend, Chief Nākaikua'ana, to steal the Inamo'o firearms from Ki'ikīkī while he surfed ("he'e nalu") offshore at Makaweli.[76] With these firearms hidden away in Nākaikua'ana's care, Kaumuali'i next offered Kapua'amohu's favors to Ki'ikīkī...30 days of lying with Kapua'amohu if he would use one of the firearms to kill Keawe. Ki'ikīkī, who was very desirous of the attractive Kapua'amohu, demanded that he lie with her for 30 days first, and *then* he would kill Keawe. Kapua'amohu did not like lying with Ki'ikīkī, saying that he was "like a beast" in his affections, but she did what her husband needed her to do. Kaumual-

---

[74] Kanakahelela 1885, Wichman 2003, Croft 2012B.

[75] Joesting 1984, p. 58.

[76] Wichman 2003, pp. 99-100.

i'i then instructed Nākaikua'ana to return to Ki'ikīkī a single loaded musket. Ki'ikīkī took the musket, followed Keawe to a favorite bathing spot called Kupaniki in Kapa'a and shot him to death while he bathed. Ki'ikīkī and his brother Kāne'eku then fled by canoe to O'ahu to escape the now powerful Kaumuali'i's (and likely Kapua'amohu's) retribution. But this did not avail them, as Kaumuali'i sent the able Nākaikua'ana to O'ahu after them. He was ordered not to return until he had found and killed them both.[77] He returned seven years later, telling Kaumuali'i that he had accomplished his task.

KAUMUALI'I BECOMES KAUAI'S GOD KING:

Kaumuali'i was, then, by the end of 1796, Kaua'i's undisputed ali'i nui. He immediately surrounded himself with only the most loyal supporters--chiefs, priests, and bodyguards. During his reign he would see no active rebellion, and very little discord. His authority, assumed before his seventeenth year, was essentially absolute. His people prostrated themselves in his presence under penalty of death, enforced by his bodyguards. Servants carried him from place to place in a litter, bearing his feather kāhili standards, his clothing,

---

[77] Croft 2012B, p. 246.

food, drink, and even his "ipu lepu," a calabash bowl to secretly dispose of his feces, hair and nail trimmings.

Being the ali'i nui meant, in the able description from Frederick B. Wichman's chapter entitled "Wā Maika'i," that he, "The paramount chief, ruled the entire island, owned all the land, and had power of life and death over all the people, ali'i (chiefs) and maka'āinana (commoners) alike. To help him govern, the ali'i nui chose a kālaimoku (prime minister; literally: "manage island"...in this case Kamaholelani, his cousin) to advise him on all practical political and civil matters."[78]

Kaumuali'i moved his primary seat of power from Wailua to Waimea on the south shore of Kaua'i, but kept high advisors in the Wailua residences to respond to political and religious concerns. Wichman continues: "Both ali'i and maka'āinana young men were kept as a standing army, vigorously trained in all the martial arts. To keep interest lively, these athletes displayed their skills and bravery in frequent pageants and tournaments where betting took on a punitive aspect. Genealogists, historians, storytellers, and hula groups kept the royal court entertained. A horde of commoners kept daily life operating smoothly.

---

[78] "Good Times," Wichman 2003, pp. 53-55.

Kaua'i was divided into six "moku" ("districts"), which were governed by ali'i 'ai moku (chief who leads the land), each carefully chosen for his loyal-

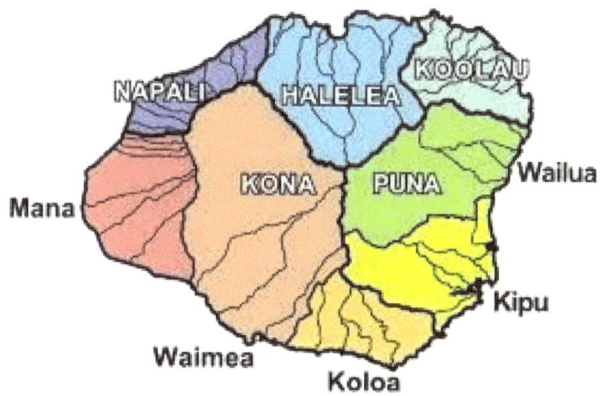

The Moku (Districts) of Kaua'i: Kona, Puna, Ko'olau, Halele'a, Nāpali. The sixth moku, the island of Ni'ihau is not shown. From: www.islandbreath.orgwww.islandbreath.org. See also www.kauainuikuapapa.com for the ahupua'as' (shown here) names.

ty and close relationship with the ruling king (ali'i nui). The largest district was Kona, the former kingdom now centered in Waimea, followed in size by Puna. Ko'olau, the land between the Makaleha mountains and the sea that faced the northeast trade winds contained the least amount of water but had a teeming reef along its shores. Halele'a, with its spectacular mountains and waterfalls, and Nāpali of the western-facing valleys surrounded by two-thousand-feet cliffs and the ocean, are the most spectacular. The island of Ni'ihau (the sixth district...author) was historically populated from Kaua'i during years of sufficient rainfall and abandoned when drought beset it," but in Kaumuali'i's time a permanent population remained there for him to govern.

(Continuing from Wichman): The ali'i 'ai moku was responsible for the well-being of his district and for passing on to the ali'i nui the prescribed amount of food, from taro to pigs, from bananas to fish. He also sent food and such manufactured necessities of life that the people in his district produced."

In addition, each of the six moku under Kaumuali'i's rule was composed of smaller, pie-shaped land units called "ahupua'a" (prefectures), each reaching from the central mountain tops and extending down streams between two ridges clear out across the beaches and into the deep-sea fishing grounds offshore. The district chief appointed a "konohiki" (tax chief) to be in charge of each ahupua'a. The families living there had access to all the resources of the ahupua'a, including "lo'i" (taro fields) and dry land "māla" (farming fields) and fish ponds. In return the ahupua'a inhabitants had to work on a fixed part-time schedule in fields and ponds set aside for the government.

Once a year, usually at the start of the "makahiki" (holiday and harvest) season in the fall and winter, the commoners paid a tax in the form of goods: pigs, dogs, chickens, vegetables, fish, mats and baskets, woven cordage, nets, paddles, tools, wooden calabashes, gourds, and, above all, feathers from the colorful birds for the cloaks, leis, and helmets used to indicate ali'i status.

(Further from Wichman): "Since the ali'i nui was considered the personal representative, as well as the direct descendent, of the gods on earth, it was natural that he owned all the land with all the living things upon it, including the people who could not and did not own anything. The ali'i nui had the awesome responsibility to perform the proper prayers and present the proper offerings (including people…author) to the gods to ensure the well-being of all. He was supported by his "kahuna nui" (head priest), who advised him on all religious matters."

So, as ali'i nui, Kaumuali'i headed a political and religious administration of ali'i for Kaua'i's six moku and their 55 composing ahupua'a.[79] The administering ali'i under Kaumuali'i did not work. Nor did their direct families work. All were sustained by the work of the commoners they ruled.

---

[79] see http://kauainuikuapapa.com for the names of the ahupua'a in each moku.

And there were many ali'i to be so sustained…not only the high chiefs and their families, but their subordinate chiefs and their families, the priests and their families, the mū bodyguards, the chanters, historians, genealogists, storytellers… It is easy to estimate that the thirty thousand people that ali'i nui Kaumuali'i reckoned were living in his kingdom of Kaua'i (see below) were toiling hard every day to support the thousand or so people privileged to be in their god king's government structure. And, there was the constant possibility of their being forced to fight in the army (women too) or even sacrificed by the ali'i nui and his priests to the gods for some kapu-infringement or crime.

KAMEHAMEHA PLANS A SECOND ATTACK ON KAUA'I:

By 1804, after eight years of solidifying his authority over the other islands, Kamehameha began the assembly of another great army on O'ahu, intending a second amphibious assault on adjacent Kaua'i. This time his army included over 7,000 Hawaiian and 50 European soldiers, most armed with muskets. They were equipped with 6 mortars, 8 heavy cannon, 40 swivel guns, 21 armed schooners, and a very large fleet of double-hulled canoes. When Kaumuali'i was informed of these preparations, both by Chief Nākaikua'ana upon his return from his long murder-mission in O'ahu and by English Captain John Turnbull, who had seen them, he realized that he would only be able to muster a third of Kamehameha's armed force to defend Kaua'i.[80]

Kaumuali'i understood that Kamehameha would, in victory, slaughter and sacrifice him, his family, and his chiefs as he had done on his previously conquered islands. And he knew that the people of Kaua'i would also be killed in large numbers, both during the conflict as soldiers and afterwards when Kamehameha's chiefs took advantage of them in new ways. Because of this, Kaumuali'i commenced days and days of isolated prayer, requesting his gods to confound Kamehameha's plans. And he ordered the immediate construction by some Kaua'i-resident foreign beachcombers of a western-style sailing vessel on which he could make an escape to another Pacific island or even China.

RESCUED BY DISEASE—THE SQUATTING SICKNESS:

But for Kaumuali'i an escape was not needed. Kamehameha's forces were struck down severely by a disease they called "ma'i 'ōku'u," or squatting sickness. This was apparently a type of

---

[80] Daws 1974, p. 42, Joesting 1984, p. 62.

cholera, and it quickly devastated the assembled forces, killing and "blackening the bodies" of a thousand or more, including several of Kamehameha's closest chiefs. Ke'eaumoku, the father of Kamehameha's favorite wife Ka'ahumanu and the man who had thrown the spear killing Keoua, Kamehameha's one-time rival for control of Hawai'i Island, died of the sickness in Kamehameha's presence. Kamehameha was seriously sickened himself and barely survived, so that he was shaken out of continuing this invasion of Kaua'i. When Russian Captain Yurii Lisiansky of the *Neva*, which reached Kaua'i on 19 June of 1804, reported the results of this horrific pestilence to Kaumuali'i, Kaumuali'i was greatly relieved and jubilantly told Lisiansky that Kamehameha's failure was no doubt due to his prayers, and that his island, "over thirty thousand strong," was also "Kaua'i pule o'o," Kaua'i of strong prayer.

KAMEHAMEHA NEGOTIATES WITH KAUMUALI'I:

Kamehameha did not give up on his intention to add Kaua'i and Ni'ihau to his domain. He merely changed his method, deciding to negotiate Kaumuali'i and his islands into tributary status. Several delegations of chiefs (e.g. by Kihei, Wahine, Pakiko, and Kamaholelani) were sent back and forth between Kamehameha and Kaumuali'i. One of these O'ahu chiefs, Kihei, was so positively impressed with Kaumuali'i's "kinder rule" on Kaua'i that he decided not to return to Kamehameha's realm, but instead remain on Kaua'i, loyal to Kaumuali'i. Kaumuali'i gave him wives and land.

KAUMUALI'I CHOOSES PEACE FOR KAUA'I:

At last, in April of 1810, after five years of negotiations, Kaumuali'i was persuaded to come to Honolulu to meet Kamehameha face-to-face. Kamehameha sent his close English advisor Isaac Davis and his chiefs Keawe'opu and Nahili on Boston Captain Nathan Winship's brig *Albatross*[81] to collect Kaumuali'i and his party, which included his wife Namahana and their three-year-old son Kahekili, as well as high chief and "kālaimoku" (prime minister) Kamaholelani and the youngest and newest of Kaumuali'i's wives, his then favorite, Kekaiha'akulou. Captain Winship's first mate, William Smith, agreed to stay behind on Kaua'i as a hostage to assure that Kaumuali'i and his party would safely return.

On the way to Honolulu, Kaumuali'i spoke at length in English with Isaac Davis, with whom he got along quite agreeably. He told Davis and Cap-

---

[81] See Howay 1932, pp. 43-86 with other sources about the ship.

tain Winship also, that he had been persuaded to become Kamehameha's "Ali'i moku," meaning still a king of Kaua'i, but a vassal to the Hawaiian

Sketch of Kamehameha I ("The Great") (1758?-8 May, 1819) by Louis Choris (1795-1828) in 1816, from: http://www.nps.gov/puhe/historyculture/Kamehameha.htm, also from: http://en.wikipedia.org/wiki/Kamehameha_I

islands' overall ruler, Kamehameha. He agreed to this, he said, because "otherwise so many many will die…not only my family, my chiefs, my soldiers, my people…but many of Kamehameha's people also." "In these islands," he said, "it is time at last for a peaceful rule. No more war." Both Isaac Davis and Captain Winship congratulated Kaumuali'i, telling him that they thought he was doing, "the right thing."

In Honolulu harbor, the *Albatross* was anchored and the crew watched a large group of feather-cloaked Hawaiian chiefs approach the ship from shore in their canoes. But Kamehameha arrived by surprise alone in a smaller canoe from the ocean side, and when he, in all his official regalia and carrying a small pig in his arms as a token, climbed over the gunwale onto the main deck, he said to Kaumuali'i, similarly attired, "E homai ko lima" (Give me your hand). Kaumuali'i reached out to grasp Kamehameha's hand and asked him pointedly "Will it be face up, or face down?" Kamehameha put down the pig, which scrambled straight to Kaumuali'i's feet, and then responded, "There is no death."[82]

The details of this event…especially Kamehameha's bringing a baby pig with him in his regalia… may be hard to interpret. But scholars of Hawaiian

---

[82] John Papa Ii 1995, p. 82, Zambucka 1999, p. 25.

history and religion opine that Kamehameha, in fear of the dreaded "ane'ekapuahi" prayer that had once apparently caused the incineration of the foreign cannoneer Mare Amara, had sought counsel with his head priest, his kingdom's "kahuna nui," the pope-like Hewahewa, about how to protect himself. Hewahewa had carefully blessed the baby pig and told Kamehameha that it would run to whomever in his presence had uttered such a destructive prayer against him, and that this identification would foil the praying person's intent so that "There is no death".[83]

In a few minutes of conversation the meaning of this unique exchange became clear to all. Kamehameha meant no harm to Kaumuali'i and agreed to let Kaumuali'i rule Kaua'i and Ni'ihau with his chiefs "as he had been until the end of his days." But then the rule would pass not to Kaumuali'i's intended successor, his son Keali'iahonui, but to Kamehameha's heir and designated successor, Liholiho, his oldest son from his "Sacred Queen," Keōpūolani. As a sign of his sincerity, Kamehameha presented to Kaumuali'i a really splendid red feathered mahiole cap, and, even more significant, the fabled "Ka 'ei kapu o Liloa,"

---

[83] See Gutmanis 1983, pp. 27-8 for defenses against pule 'ana'ana or "death prayers" involving a pig, and also Kamakau 1964, Part VI about "Magic and Sorcery," pp. 118-141, esp. p. 121.

a red-and-gold-feathered body-sash, with 69 individual human molars sewn into its end tassels, that had once belonged to Liloa, Kamehameha's fifteenth-century predecessor as ruler of Hawai'i

Hawaiian artist and historian **Brook Kapūkuniahi Parker** in the Bishop Museum holding the original Mahiole cap given to Kaumuali'i by Kamehameha in 1810.

Island, and was emblematic of a king reputedly munificent. These objects are displayed to this day in Honolulu's Bishop Museum's Hawaiian Hall. [84]

KAUMUALI'I ESCAPES FROM O'AHU:

After the official agreement had been concluded, Kamehameha invited Kaumuali'i and his party to come ashore for a celebration. Foreigners' rum would be served. But Isaac Davis warned Kaumuali'i in English that he and his party should not attend, because some of Kamehameha's chiefs, disappointed with the agreement, intended to poison them. Oral legends then tell of how Kaumuali'i and Kekaiha'akulou had to "escape" from Honolulu by traveling at night northward through an area known as Lihue to the north shore of O'ahu, where they found outrigger canoes to get them home by paddling and sailing across the difficult channel. One can only imagine how glad Captain Winship's first mate John Williams, the hostage kept on Kaua'i to assure Kaumuali'i's safety, was to see them return. The *Albatross* had arrived off Waimea the previous day without Kaumuali'i, causing Williams real concern.

---

[84] See the similar "malo" in Ii 1995, p.28. But only 39 molars. Also note the "Cordon of Kaumualii" (sic) pictured in Zambucka 1999, p. 66. The above pictured cap is also shown in Kirch 2012, plate 6 after p. 142.

At the "celebration" of the agreement on O'ahu, Isaac Davis was himself then poisoned by the disappointed chiefs, and died the next day. Kamehameha was very angered by this and asked his other English advisor John Young, a close friend of Isaac Davis's, to care for Davis's wife and children. But Kamehameha was true to his word to Kaumuali'i. He would not attack Kaua'i again, and their agreement for a change in succession upon Kaumuali'i's death would stay in effect. Kaua'i and Ni'ihau were now *de facto* parts of Kamehameha's domain and his legacy, and the year 1810 is today given as the date of the State of Hawaii's unification.

TRANQUILITY AND PROFITABILITY FOR KAUA'I:

For the next five years, Kaumuali'i did well economically on Kaua'i by selling its valuable "'iliahi," the sandalwood, to ships' captains from the United States and Great Britain, who were at that time enemies in their War of 1812, and to the captains of the Russian-American Company whose government-chartered fur business under Manager Alexander Baranov was headquartered in Sitka, Alaska. The sandalwood trade enabled Kaumuali'i to acquire diverse materiel, including western weapons.

THE RUSSIAN ADVENTURE—DR. GEORGE ANTON SCHAEFFER:

In October of 1815, Manager Alexander Baranov sent the ship *Isabella* under Captain Charles Tyler from Novoarkhangelsk (now Sitka), Alaska,

Alexander Andreevich Baranov (1746-April 19, 1819), the "Governor of Russian America," from: http://www.netstate.com/states/peop/ak_aab.htm.

to the Hawaiian Islands in order to bring back to him the cargo of his Captain James Bennett's *Bering* that had washed aground on its side during the previous winter in Waimea on Kaua'i's south shore.

On the *Isabella*, in addition to its captain and crew, were: the *Bering*'s Captain James Bennett who had been rescued from the foundered and salvaged ship, a Russian-speaking German physician, Dr. George Anton Schaeffer, Manager Baranov's nineteen-year-old Aleut-Russian son Antipatr, twenty-five Aleut seal hunters, and fifteen Russian sailors. Of these Dr. George Anton Schaeffer (1779-1836) was of the most consequence to Hawaiian history.

Dr. Schaeffer had been deliberately stranded in Sitka by Captain Mikhail Lazarev of the circum-navigating Russian Navy ship *Suvorov*, on which Dr. Schaeffer, a Russian-American Company stockholder, had served as the ship's surgeon. Previously, in the summer of 1812 in Moscow, he had been the administrator of a secret project of the Russian Tsar Alexander I to construct a gigantic shark-shaped, hydrogen-filled, rotor-wing-powered balloon, from which timed-fuse explosives were to be dropped on Napoleon Bonaparte and his marshals as they invaded Russia with their half-million-man *grande armée*.[85]

Now Russian-American Company Manager Baranov had another challenging commission for Dr. Schaeffer to accomplish. He wanted Dr.

This is the Ardis Hertford portrait of Dr. "Georg Anton Schaffer" from 1845 that hangs in the Kaua'i Museum in Lihue, Hawaii. From: http://en.wikipedia.org/wiki/Georg_Anton_Schaffer

---

[85] Croft 2012A.

Schaeffer not only to effect the return of the *Bering's* cargo from Kaumuali'i on Kaua'i, but also to gain a "foothold," a "provisioning outpost" of substance in the more temperate and fertile Hawaiian Islands. Baranov thought that Dr. Schaeffer could do this by prevailing upon King Kamehameha, then living at his new capital back on his home island of Hawai'i at Kailua. Manager Baranov and King Kamehameha had, through emissaries and translated letters,[86] though they had never personally met, come strangely to think of each other as kindred souls who had survived incredible trials in their quite parallel lives through the many years. They were, Baranov told Dr. Schaeffer in Russian, "starye druz'ja," ("old friends").

KA'AHUMANU GIVES DR. SCHAEFFER WAIKĪKĪ:

Dr. Schaeffer and his men arrived on Hawai'i Island at Kawaihae in order to "pass muster" with Kamehameha's English advisor and friend, John Young (called 'Olohana in Hawaiian), in November of 1815. John Young was, due to his dislike of Captain Bennett, immediately suspicious of the Russian American Company's motives in send-

---

[86] See Warne 2008, p. 56.

ing such a large party to see Kamehameha. But he accompanied them to Kamehameha's settlement in Kailua and saw that they were intro-

Sketch of John Young (1742-17 December, 1835) by Jacques Arago (1790-1855)
http://en.wikipedia.org/wiki/John_Young
(Hawaii).

duced to the King. Dr. Schaeffer handled this well and managed to be allowed to stay in guest hale near the royal residences for over four months, during which time Dr. Schaeffer studied hard with native aid and learned to speak Hawaiian with surprising facility.[87]

Dr. Schaeffer became acquainted with Kamehameha's minister chiefs and his queens, notably his formidable favorite, Ka'ahumanu. With Antipatr Baranov, a German-born American nephew of wealthy entrepreneur John Jacob Astor named John Marshall, and a native guide, he climbed up to the summit of dormant volcano Mauna Kea… among the first Europeans to do so. He won favor by using a colchicine tea to alleviate Kamehameha's gout. So successful was he at his ingratiation of the King and his queens that Queen Ka'ahumanu personally escorted him and his men on the British ship *Beverly* to O'ahu and gave him a "pay-it-when-you-get-it" lease on the land from the "wizard stones" to "Le'ahi" (Diamond Head) extending back to the Ko'olau Mountain ridge. In short, all of current Waikīkī and more was his.[88] And she assigned thirty families of O'ahu maka'āinana to help Dr. Schaeffer and his men build and operate their "outpost in Hawaii." Only did Ka'ahumanu caution him about Kamehameha's "three main kapus for foreigners allowed to operate on his land:" 1) Do not build any stone structures; 2) Do not fly any foreign flags over

---

[87] Croft 2012B, p. 7. Dr. Schaeffer was a gifted acquirer of foreign language abilities.

[88] See Pierce 1976, p. 164.

Hawaiian soil; and 3) Do not cut down any sandalwood.

Sketch of Ka'ahumanu's face (1768-5 June, 1832) by Louis Choris (1795-1828) in 1816, from: http://en.wikipedia.org/wiki/Louis_Choris.

DR. SCHAEFFER GOES TO KAUA'I:

Quite soon Dr. Schaeffer had trouble with the congregation of U.S. and British Captains in nearby Honolulu. They were no longer at war with each other by the end of 1815 and cooperatively agreed that they didn't want any Russian commercial competition. They conspired to inform John Young and Kamehameha that Dr. Schaeffer and his men were violating all three of the kapus they had been given on O'ahu. By May of 1816, Dr. Schaeffer had welcomed the Russian-American-Company ship *Otkrytie* (named in Russian "Discovery" as were named full-rigged ships of both Captains James Cook and George Vancouver) under Russian Captain Yakov Podushkin to Honolulu, and the resident U.S. and British Captains feared the increase in Dr. Schaeffer's available manpower. An open conflict with an inspecting John Young in early May of 1816 caused Dr. Schaeffer to sail with about half his men on the *Otkrytie* to Kaua'i, where King Kaumuali'i welcomed him enthusiastically.[89]

DR. SCHAEFFER AND KAUMUALI'I—THE "FRIENDS GEORGE:"

Kaumuali'i had educated himself well on the foreigners' international politics. He had already

---

[89] Croft 2012B, pp. 233-235.

taken clever advantage of the War of 1812 between England and the United States in his dealings with their sea captains, fur traders, and sandalwood merchants. And he was aware of these countries' recent perception of Russia as a powerful nation ruled by an able Tsar. The arrival of Dr. Schaeffer on a Russian-American Company ship with so many Russians aboard, presented to him an opportunity to change his beloved Kaua'i from a tributary island in Kamehameha's realm to a position of dominance in the inter-island politics. Especially with the forceful Kamehameha now growing old, Kaumuali'i saw a chance that the Russian government of Tsar Alexander I, the mighty "conqueror of Napoleon" in Europe, and with a prominent Russian commercial enterprise in the Pacific, might provide him with a way to cancel advantageously his forced 1810 agreement to cede posthumously his islands to Kamehameha's successor.

As Kaumuali'i thought about it, he realized that he might even be able to use Russian military might, or the threat of such might, to take over Kamehameha's rule on the other islands as well. This seemed outrageously ambitious, but he did, after all, have a more powerful genealogical "mana" than Kamehameha, and the gods had treated him well in the past due to his great powers of prayer. So right from the start of their relationship, he went along with his "Friend George's," i.e. Dr.

Schaeffer's, constant onslaught of grandiose ingratiations. Dr. Schaeffer inducted Kaumuali'i into the Russian Navy as an officer and gave him a silver dirk and a dress uniform. Dr. Schaeffer requested that he scribe his sign (an "X" or a scribed mo'o gecko lizard...his "aumakua" (patron animal spirit)) on all manner of paper treaties and documents of agreement witnessed by many of his chiefs and his queens. These treaties and documents were attestations of Kaumuali'i's formal placing of his entire kingdom into a "Russian Protectorate." They gave to Russia and its agent, Dr. Schaeffer, exclusive trading rights for Kaua'i's valuable sandalwood and other natural crops and products.

After an afternoon of document signing on board the *Otkrytie*, at 5:00 pm on the 21st of May, 1816 by the Russian calendar (13 days behind the Western European Calendar in the nineteenth century in the Pacific...before there was an international dateline), Dr. Schaeffer asked Kaumuali'i, as a sign of his agreement to accept the protection of the Russian Tsar Alexander I (which, of course, he had no authorization to do) to fly the Russian flag over his capital. He then gave Kaumuali'i a folded Russian flag and had him rowed ashore in one of the ship's boats. Within an hour he watched the Russian flag hoisted above Waimea. He then gave the ship's Captain, Ivan

Podushkin, the order to have a fourteen-shot cannon salute fired in celebration.[90]

The next day, King Kaumuali'i put on a great feast for Dr. Schaeffer and most of the Russian ship's crew at his residence Papa'ena'ena on the hillside "mauka" (inland) of Waimea village. The banquet featured low western-style tables with sixty-two short stools and the King's high-backed chair at the end as a kind of throne. Bottles of rum and glass tumblers were at each guest's table space. The main fare was roast dog, of which thirty had been provided. But there was also pork and fish, and both fresh water and ocean shrimp. Decorative clusters of bananas were piled in the center of the tables. Dr. Schaeffer was introduced to more than ten of Kaumuali'i's chiefs, to seven of his wives, and three of his children. But only a few of the chiefs and none of the wives and children ate with the Russian guests. They watched from a short distance away, as did more than four hundred, by the Russians' estimate, Waimea villagers. Horseback riding was exhibited for the guests' entertainment, and Dr. Schaeffer's Aleuts responded by putting on a drum-accompanied group dance.

At the Waimea celebration, according to Dr. Schaeffer's Russian journal, Kaumuali'i informed him that he had ordered a luakini heiau to be built

---

[90] Pierce 1976, pp. 63-65.

on a piece of land on the east bank of the Waimea River near its confluence with the ocean. This was a place, Kaumuali'i said, where Dr. Schaeffer would be given land. And Dr. Schaeffer reported Kaumuali'i as telling him, "we sacrificed two 'kauwā' outcasts to be placed beneath the heiau. As is our custom, their left eyeballs were cut out for me to consume…but I only pretend to eat them as we are not cannibals. It is part of the ritual of commissioning the sacrifices…giving them duties to perform for us in the spirit world. One of them is to act in the spirit world to help you, and the other is to help me…against the warlike spirit of Kamehameha."[91]

During the next year, Dr. Schaeffer had conversations with King Kaumuali'i quite often. He became a *de facto* regent of Kaua'i…a kind of secondary partner in the island's rule, superceding all of Kaumuali'i's chiefs except, perhaps, Kamaholelani in his authority. In the course of this year, he designed and supervised the construction for Kaumuali'i of three armed forts: the lava rock "Fort Elizaveta" (Waimea's "Russian Fort") named for the Tsar's consort on the land atop the elevated bank on the Waimea River mouth's eastern shore adjacent to the Pā'ula'ula o hipo heiau, with cannons whose field of fire covered the offshore an-

---

[91] Croft 2012, p. 200. See Te Rangi Hiroa (Buck) 1957, p. 2.

chorage; a high bluff-top earthen fort named "Fort Alexander" after the Tsar, and just below it another earthen "Fort Barclay" named after the Russian General Barclay de Tolly, hero of the Battle of Borodino against Napoleon.[92] The latter forts had their guns covering Hanalei Bay. Today the berm outline of Fort Alexander is located at the very entrance to Kaua'i's grand St. Regis hotel, with a small explanatory pavilion for tourists. The remains of Fort Barclay on the other side of the Hanelei River near the present day pier have been leveled by house construction of private residences on Weke Road in the first decade of this millenium.

Dr. Schaeffer set about creating for Kaumuali'i a "Kaua'i Navy" by committing Russian-American-Company ships and purchasing others with purchase agreements he sent to Governor Baranov in Sitka. Soon the navy had five western-rigged ships at its disposal (i.e. *Kadiak, Otkrytie, Avon, Il'mena, and Lydia*) and had plans to acquire several more.[93] In gratitude for this, Kaumuali'i and his chiefs and queens commenced to grant Dr. Schaeffer and certain of his men lands and families to work those lands. Kaumuali'i ceded to Dr. Schaeffer personally all of the north shore of Kaua'i from Ke'e Beach to Anini, including all of Hanalei,

---

[92] Croft 2012A, pp. 232-234, 246-254 Borodino.

[93] Ibid, pp. 224-238.

which Schaeffer renamed "Schefferthal" after Kaumuali'i suggested he give Russian place names to his new possessions, saying "The names are part of the spirit of the places, you know."[94] Dr. Schaeffer wrote to his wife and daughter in St. Petersburg a letter in which he described the grand stone house he planned to build for them on the bluff near Fort Alexander (above the "Queen's Bath" in present day Princeville). All this as a consequence of Dr. Schaeffer's promise to deliver Russian military might to the Pacific…essentially a Russian "adoption" of Hawaii, which he had only an inflated opinion of his ability to get enacted.

Dr. George Anton Schaeffer and King Kaumuali'i communicated in both Hawaiian and in English. They called each other "Friend George" although George spelled Kaumuali'i's name in his log in the Russian equivalent of "Tamoree." Other Hawaiians called Dr. Schaeffer "Kepa" as he ministered to them medically (he amputated a warrior's leg, medicated away gout with colchicine tea, pulled decayed or abcessed teeth, helped in problem births…and such). The close personal relationship that the two leaders developed over the fourteen months from May 1816 to July 1817 was unique among such European-Hawaiian contacts, with the sole exception of John Young and Kamehameha. Dr. Schaeffer and Kaumuali'i were very

---

[94] Ibid, p. 238.

close to the same age (Schaeffer, born in Munnerstadt, Germany, in January of 1779, was a year older, they together determined). They were both physically robust individuals with forceful prepossessing personalities. Both were, in their own ways, religious men (Dr. Schaeffer was a Catholic who had memorized the "Lord's Prayer" in Don Francisco de Paula Marin's Hawaiian translation[95]) who believed in the power of prayer…though to different gods. Both were clearly gifted learners with prodigious memories who believed in the value of education to building a society more pleasant to live in.

TIMOFEI TARAKANOV AND HIS "KAUWĀ" FAMILY:

Kaumuali'i wanted his younger son Kahekili, then about ten years old, to learn the Russian language. He said he planned for Kahekili to represent Kaua'i in the "Tsar's court" someday.[96] So Dr. Schaeffer turned the instruction task over to his literate assistant, Timofei Tarakanov, a seasoned Alaskan seal hunter who impressed Kaumuali'i with son Kahekili's progress so that he gave Tarakanov "a village with thirteen families, on the

---

[95] Ibid p. 163.

[96] Ibid p. 251.

left bank of the Don River (Dr. Schaeffer renamed the Hanapēpē River the "Don" after the River in Ukraine) in the province (ahupua'a) of Hanapēpē"[97] as a reward and allowed him to live there with a Hawaiian woman he renamed "Lara" of the "kauwā" caste of pariah[98] and her two children, a girl he called "Ninochka" and a boy "Koli," after her husband had been killed by a thrown stone while attempting to steal a villager's dog in Waikīkī on O'ahu.[99]

DR. SCHAEFFER OPPOSES SACRIFICING HUMANS:

In July of 1816 Kaumuali'i invited Dr. Schaeffer, Timofei Tarakanov, and four others of their company to accompany him on a tour of Kaua'i's southeast shore. In two days of following the King's warrior-borne palanquin they reached a volcanic crater called Pu'uwanawana near a village in Koloa. Here they spent half of a sunny day listening to Kaumuali'i tell them a story from

---

[97] Pierce 1976, p. 192, Croft 2012B, p. 251.

[98] Marked (tattooed) as possible sacrifice victims in Hawaiian society...see Beckwith Notes, also Malo 1997, pp. 68-72.

[99] Croft 2012B, p. 232.

Kaua'i's history. Kaumuali'i told the story in Hawaiian, loudly and with animated hand gestures and facial expressions. The narration was nevertheless a bit labored because Dr. Schaeffer needed to interrupt frequently to get clarifications from him in both Hawaiian and in English, then interpret his resultant understanding into Russian for the others.

The story was a tale of how the tall ancient King Kukona had captured four kings from other islands who had tried to conquer Kaua'i, and about how, through the supernatural agency of a big-island "kāula" (prophetess), a woman named Wa'ahia, he had come to possess a marooned Japanese warrior's metal samurai sword.[100] Dr. Schaeffer was impressed by how Kaumuali'i, before he began to tell his story, spent more than an hour alone on his mat shaded by his kāhili standards praying to his gods to make his story appropriately instructive to his guests. His purpose was to convince them that the gods favored Kaua'i's kings, both Kukona and him, because of the just ("pono") way they ruled their island. The following dialogue is imagined from Dr. Schaeffer's description of it:

"The gods are pleased with us, and they have rewarded us," Kaumuali'i said, and he gave an example: "When Kamehameha sent his many canoes

---

[100] Croft 2012B, pp. 209-218, Kalakaua 1990, pp. 175-205.

full of armed warriors to conquer Kaua'i in your year of 1796, the wind goddess La'amaomao, preferring us to Kamehameha despite his many human sacrifices, sent her son, the strong gust called Kulepe, to swamp Kamehameha's canoes in the channel between O'ahu and here.[101] The goddess La'amaomao forced Kamehameha to give up his attack on us and return to O'ahu. Many of his men drowned and we easily killed all of those who did manage to land on our shores."

"You were only, as I now reckon, sixteen years old, is that correct?" asked Dr. Schaeffer in Hawaiian.

" 'Ae (Yes), but I prayed strongly at that time too," answered Kaumuali'i. "And again in your year of 1804, I prayed to our gods that Kamehameha's second planned attack on us from O'ahu would fail. And the gods, despite Kamehameha's sacrificing a great number of O'ahu's men, made him and his warriors terribly ill with the squatting disease ("ma'i 'ōku'u"). Once again my prayers were rewarded by the gods."

"I would think from this that Kamehameha's human sacrifices did not please the gods as much as your prayers," said Dr. Schaeffer. "I would even think that his sacrifices of people in such numbers displeased the gods so that they punished

---

[101] See Kawaharada 1992 site.

him and his warriors. The gods see him having people killed, and they hear you pray. From what you tell us, they clearly prefer what they hear. Do you not think so?"

"In my rule too, Friend George, people have been sacrificed," answered Kaumuali'i. "But always for a pono reason, and even so…less and less in these days."

"For what reasons have you sacrificed people?" asked Dr. Schaeffer.

"Do you remember that young warrior whose leg you cut off after it was mangled in taking ashore one of your ship's cannons?" asked Kaumuali'i.

"Yes, I remember," answered Dr. Schaeffer. "I saw him in Waimea only three days ago walking on the stump I fashioned for him. I didn't think he would survive the fever he got after his leg was gone. And he had lost a terrible amount of blood."

"His life was more important to us than the life of another man we all knew to be a thief," answered Kaumuali'i. "And so I ordered the thief sacrificed. And the pleased gods gave strength to my young warrior. And now the warrior lives."

"So it's a life for a life in exchange, is that it?"

"Sometimes a single life sacrificed will save many," Kaumuali'i said. "Do you remember just last moon when that strong storm broke your ship's main mast on your way to Ni'ihau and you tried to find help there to get it repaired? And then you set about to paddle your way back to Waimea in a small seal-skin baidarka with two of your men? Why do you think the ship was repaired and how were you allowed to make it back safely to Waimea? And how did we in Waimea lose only one old man when the storm destroyed most of the village? It all came out well because I had been making the sacrifices that were enough to please the gods, so that they helped you too. They made the Ni'ihau konohiki help your shipmates, they pacified the channel waves for your baidarka, and they had the winds spare our villagers while taking down almost every hale and heiau tower in Waimea."

"Let me tell you about my own all-powerful God, Jehovah," said Dr. Schaeffer.

"I would very much like to hear about your god, Friend George," said Kaumuali'i. "I have already heard some things about him from my other foreign friends."

"Well this is about how our God once asked an ancestor of ours from a very long time ago…a man named Abraham...to sacrifice his only son Isaac to him by burning Isaac up in a fire. Abraham was very strong in his commitment to God and set about to obey. He tied Isaac up and placed him on a sacrificial altar covered with wood so that he could set his son's body on fire. But just as Abraham raised his arm with a knife to slay his son, our God Jehovah called out to him from Heaven and told him to stop. 'Just knowing that you would not hold thine only son from me is enough,' God told Abraham. And God made a ram appear before Abraham so that Abraham could sacrifice this animal to God instead of his human son. And ever after that, our God has not required a human sacrifice of anyone except his own son Jesus whom he sent to save us all forever from our sinful ways. The people who follow our God can make all kinds of other sacrifices to Him, but our people themselves are sacred to God and should not be sacrificed by any earthly ruler."

"I thank you for that good story, Friend George," Kaumuali'i said. "I will ask my gods about it in prayer."

Dr. Schaeffer's Russian journal records that he and Kaumuali'i forthrightly discussed human sacrifice on several other occasions, but Dr. Schaeffer did not immediately succeed in persuading Kaumuali'i to give up the practice of human sacrifice, of which Dr. Schaeffer strongly disapproved. In

September of 2016, Dr. Schaeffer made Kaumuali'i promise not to sacrifice anyone for the purpose of hallowing the construction of the new stone "Fort Elizaveta" (the "Russian Fort) in Waimea, even though it was to be built on the site of the important, Pa'ulu'ula o Hipo Heiau. And more than one of Kaumuali'i's queens, at least Namahana, Naoa (then pregnant), and Kekaiha'akulou, who were personally participating in the construction, assured him that no such sacrifice had been placed, as was the tradition, below the building's corner. Dr. Schaeffer was happy about this, and thought that he might bemaking progress with the King. But after the Fort's construction was essentially complete, Kaumuali'i asked Dr. Schaeffer to direct the construction also of a grand new King's Residence (a new "Papa'ena'ena") of stone for him just makai (seaward) of the Fort. When that was done, one of the queens told Dr. Schaeffer that two men, thought to be spies from O'ahu, had been selected for sacrifice, were killed, and their bones buried beneath the building's corner.[102]

---

[102] Croft 2012B, p. 242, and see Kanakahelela 1885, for involvement of Kaumuali'i's priests Kū'ohu and Kapu'ahi in victim selection. Also see Mills 2002, p. 105.

Brook Kapūkuniahi Parker's July 2012 sketch of Kaumuali'i's Queen Kekaiha'akulou (later Deborah Kapule) touching noses ("honi") with Dr. George Anton Schaeffer in Fort Elizaveta (The "Russian Fort") in November 1816. Notice her "lei niho palaoa" necklace and the bodyguards ("mū") with their "pūlo'ulo'u" (kapu markers).

THE RUSSIANS' "TROUBLE IN PARADISE":

In the first months of 1817 certain frictions entered into Kaumuali'i's relationship with Dr. Schaeffer and his men. For this Dr. Schaeffer blamed Kamehameha and his advisor John Young, and the

English and American Captains who, he said, were "lying" about him and his intentions. But there were other, more local frictions also, from a few of Kaumuali'i's jealous chiefs. When Dr. Schaeffer once complained that one of his company of Aleuts was killed at his earth-work Fort Barclay in Hanalei by marauding warriors of Kaumuali'i's Chief Kaela (whom Dr. Schaeffer had renamed "Chief Vorontsov" after a prominent Russian nobleman) and that Kaumuali'i's Ali'i Aimoku Kamaholelani had refused to do anything about it, Kaumuali'i responded by having Kamaholelani present to Dr. Schaeffer a wooden box in which were four human eyeballs…intending them to be considered those of the two warriors who were guilty of killing Dr. Schaeffer's comrade.[103]

On April 23, 1817 on the Russian calendar, Dr. Schaeffer wrote up a "Trade Agreement" giving him, as agent for the Russian-American Company, exclusive rights to all of Kaua'i's commercial products. The first provision of this agreement stated (in Russian) that "King Kaumuali'i shall not trade in any articles with anybody but the Russians, unless he has the consent of Dr. Schaeffer or his successor."[104] He explained the agreement to Kaumuali'i in both Hawaiian and in English and asked him to sign it before signing witnesses

---

[103] Croft 2012B p. 277-279.

[104] Ibid, p. 292, also Pierce 1976, pp. 86-87.

Kamaholelani and Timofei Tarakanov. Kaumuali'i was clearly reluctant for the first time to sign one of Dr. Schaeffer's documents, but he eventually did so and the men all thereafter smoked a pipe together and drank 'awa as a sign of their agreement. In their conversation, Kaumuali'i mentioned the pressures upon him to disavow his agreements with the Russians: Kamehameha and John Young, the American and English captains, and some of his own chiefs, all wanted him to "steer a non-Russian course" for Kaua'i. I conjecture that a dialogue between Kaumuali'i and Dr. Schaeffer might well have gone as follows.

"You and I have discussed many things, Friend George," Kaumuali'i said. "But you should know that I do not agree with some of the plans you have for my islands and my people. You speak of changing our belief in our gods, putting a kapu on the ali'i, teaching our children to read and write Russian, paying our maka'āinana for their work, and other disturbing things. In some ways, these notions are as threatening to us as Kamehameha and his warriors. How am I to rule when faced with such a threat of strange and foreign ideas?"[105]

"There is only one God you should worry about," answered Dr. Schaeffer, "and that is the God Jehovah of whom I have told you. And you

---

[105] Ibid, p. 294.

ali'i have long been in the process of killing each other until someday soon there will be none left. And there will be no kapus either. In this modern world the rule of kings depends upon the people they rule. And these people will work better if they can read and write and if they are not slaves, but are given something of value to them in exchange for their work."

"The people do whatever I want done because they know that I and my prayers protect them and allow them to live in peace," answered Kaumuali'i. "You know that my prayers give me the ability to affect not only what people do, but also what you call nature does. My prayers protect my people from storms. They are why we have no volcanoes erupting here on Kaua'i like they do on Hawai'i. They assure the people plenty of all their crops and of fish and prevent them from starving. I pray to the gods for my people every day. But the gods require me to make sacrifices to them to earn their help for us all. I give them all kinds of offerings, but for the most important things they want me to sacrifice people."

"How do your gods tell you this?" asked Dr. Schaeffer. "Do they appear to you as people? Do you hear voices speaking to you?"

"No, Friend George," answered Kaumuali'i. "Our gods are more than just people. They don't speak to me in people's voices. They simply arrange my thoughts while I am in prayer with them and I know what they want from me. I understand them because of my mana."

"I see," answered Dr. Schaeffer. "And I must say that compared to the other ali'i I've known or heard about, you are a king who cares more about the people you rule, and that is a good thing. You want your people to learn, for example…to become educated about things so that they can better take care of themselves and their children. Did your gods instruct you in this?"

"My gods and my mother," answered Kaumuali'i. "And some foreigners like you. You and I have talked about founding schools for Kaua'i's children where teachers teach them to read and write. And I do agree that their learning to read and write is a good thing…but when we have such schools, can we not teach our children to read and write in their own language instead of Russian?"

"I do admit that would be a good thing, and that it could be possible too," answered Dr. Schaeffer. "If you want I could write up some other agreements that would enable the changes that YOU want. Do you want me to do that?"

"I think I've signed enough of your agreements now, Friend George," answered Kaumuali'i. "I don't need such agreements to make the changes I want."

FRICTION BECOMES FIRE:

By May of 1817 Kaumuali'i realized that he would have to disassociate himself from Dr. Schaeffer and his "Russian Protectorate." To accomplish this, he simply began to diminish Dr. Schaeffer's access to him. This disaffection was most clearly evidenced to Dr. Schaeffer when, on May 8, 1817, he saw that the Russian flag, which Kaumuali'i had earlier refused to strike when British and American Captains had demanded he do so, had been replaced by a flag, apparently of his own design...a horizontally hung rectangle divided into alternating white and blue triangles with four black circles clustered in the center.[106] And when Dr. Schaeffer and Timofei Tarakanov were at last forcibly expelled from Waimea (Kaumuali'i gave Tarakanov permission to fetch his family from Hanapēpē), one of Dr. Schaeffer's men, Englishman Charles Fox-Bennick, who had been teaching English to Queen Kekaiha'akulou, was "chosen for

---

[106] See sketch from Dr. Schaeffer's journal in Pierce 1976, p. 200. Also, it's blue and white diagonally crossed rectangle resembles the Russian Navy Ensign.

sacrifice" and tortured on shore by being gradually hung by the neck until Kekaiha'akulou and her bodyguards showed up to free him and gave him a boat to row himself out to the Russians' ship *Kadiak*. There Dr. Schaeffer and his men had been preparing a cannon to "put him out of his misery."[107] I can find no written evidence that Kekaiha'akulou, after becoming a Christian under the name of Deborah Kapule, ever told anyone of this story. We don't know if Kaumuali'i himself ordered the strangulation torture of Fox-Bennick...Dr. Schaeffer suspected the jealous chiefs or angry priests... but, with only a word, Kaumuali'i surely could have stopped his young wife and queen from rescuing her former English instructor. He apparently chose not to do so, staying well out of sight. That is perhaps evidence that Kaumuali'i felt some compunction about the need to disassociate himself from his "Friend George" and his Russian-American Company associates.[108]

DR. SCHAEFFER FLEES HAWAII:

By July of 1817, Dr. Schaeffer was at last undone by several events. Among these was the arrival of the genuine Russian Navy ship *Rurik* at

---

[107] Croft 2012B, pp. 301-304.

[108] See also Pierce 1976, pp. 102-103.

Kamehameha's settlement at Kailua on the big island. The *Rurik's* Captain Otto von Kotsebue confidently assured Kamehameha that the Russian Tsar Alexander I was, despite Dr. Schaeffer's insistence to the contrary, clearly disinclined to make any territorial claims in the far-off Pacific. He told Kamehameha that the "Tsar never heard of George Anton Schaeffer," which was actually untrue[109] but effective in convincing Kamehameha to send his "Iron Cable," the formidable war minister Kalanimoku to Kaua'i to "have a serious talk with Kaumuali'i." This talk, which took place covertly in Wailua, was apparently quite impactful.[110]

Also, the American and British Captains came up with a strategy to spread the false rumor that the United States and Russia were at war and that, as a result, the United States would send troops to Kaua'i to evict the Russian interlopers there. And, Manager Baranov in Sitka refused to pay for ships (e.g. Captain Isaac Whitmore's *Avon*) that Dr. Schaeffer had "purchased on notes" to swell Kaumuali'i's navy.

Dr. Schaeffer and his men tried to hole up in their Hanalei forts, Alexander and Barclay, after escaping the open conflict in Waimea. They even

---

[109] See Croft 2012A: George Anton Schaeffer: Killing Napoleon From the Air in Biblio.

[110] Croft 2012B, p. 285, 292-293.

signed a pledge to fight together to stay. But then native attacks forced them to sail away...one ship, Captain Podushkin's *Otkrytie*, to Sitka, taking away a Kaua'i chief (Kaloha'aki, whom Dr. Schaeffer called "Chief Hanalei"), his wife (Mi'ikina), and two other members of his family who were loyal to Dr. Schaeffer (we don't know what happened to them thereafter), and another ship, the terribly leaky *Kadiak* with Dr. Schaeffer himself on it, to dubious sanctuary in Honolulu near where the remaining twenty denizens of his Waikīkī outpost were.

There in Honolulu Harbor during the Americans' 1817 Independence Day celebrations, his ship sinking near the shore and surrounded by threatening foes, Dr. Schaeffer's fortunes seemed at an end. But he was rescued at the last minute by an American Captain, Isaiah Lewis of the *Panther*, whose abcessed tooth he had once extracted, saving the man's life. Captain Lewis, who had taken on Dr. Schaeffer's friend John Marshall as his first mate, sailed Dr. Schaeffer and only two of his men (Russian Filip Osipov, the "toughest man," and Aleut Grigorii Iskakov, the "oldest man") for bodyguard/escorts away to Canton, China, whence other adventures awaited Dr. Schaeffer.[111]   His Waikīkī company of Russians and Aleuts under

---

[111] See Croft 2012C: George Anton Schaeffer: Shipping Germans to Brazil.

Timofei Tarakanov,[112] were rescued a month later by a ship sent from Sitka with Manager Baranov's apologies to Kamehameha about how his representative, Dr. Schaeffer, had so grossly overstepped his authority. Kaumuali'i, however, was now more firmly ensconced in his tributary status, hav-

Author Lee B. Croft with the cannon alleged to be from the Russian-American Company ship *Kadiak* (sunk at Honolulu Harbor shoreline July 5-6, 1817). Photo by Lesley Hoyt Croft, September 2011.

---

[112] See (in Russian) Зорин, А. В.

ing aroused Kamehameha's suspicions about his loyalty and his commitment to their succession agreement.

KAUMUALI'I DOES AS KAMEHAMEHA WANTS...BUT HOW?

In December of 1817, Kamehameha negotiated a deal to purchase the British armed brig *Columbia* from its Captain John Jennings for two shiploads of sandalwood, one of which was to be collected on Kaua'i as part of Kaumuali'i's agreed-upon yearly tribute. The *Columbia's* first officer Peter Corney recorded that the ship arrived off Waimea on March 17, 1818. On board were Kalanimoku and several of Kamehameha's chiefs...and also Kamehameha's "Spanish Physician," Don Francisco de Paula Marin, called "Manini."[113] With this impressive contingent of Kamehameha's government, Kaumuali'i fully cooperated in supplying the sandalwood, even though the finding, cutting, and processing of the ever-rarer sandalwood was a task that had become generally onerous to him and his chiefs even when they would be paid for it. Corney stated that Kaumuali'i told them that he was "very glad that Kamehameha had sent for the sandalwood and that he would give it up to him with pleasure." Five hundred canoes then delivered

---

[113] Gast/Conrad 1973, p. 61.

sandalwood to the *Columbia*, filling the ship by March 25. Hogs and vegetables were also put on board as tribute. Corney's description includes mention that an English flag was flying over the "Russian Fort," "…a very fine fort, mounting thirty guns… (which is) a great credit to the engineer (Dr. George Anton Schaeffer…author), sitting on a high point at the entrance of the river, and protecting the whole town." It was, he stated, used as a "dungeon" also, to "confine both white men and natives."[114]

Kaumuali'i's acquiescence to Kamehameha's mandates was strained in August of 1818 by the notorious "Bouchard Incident." Captain Hypolite (Spanish "Hipolito") Bouchard, commander of the 34-gun armed frigate *Argentina,* was a Frenchman in the service of the revolutionary government of the United Provinces of the Rio de la Plata (establishing its independence from Spain), who had sailed from Buenos Aires eastward around the Cape of Good Hope, across the Indian Ocean and into the East Indies and then into the Pacific. He was in reality a extraordinarily bold privateer who coped badly with a scurvy-decimated crew. In the Philippines he had blockaded the city of Manila in an extortion attempt. He took a Luzon-based schooner as a prize but its crew mutinied and sailed away, escaping him.

---

[114] See Mills 2002, p. 120.

When he at last reached landfall at Kealakekua Bay on the island of Hawai'i Captain Bouchard saw there an 18-gun ship, a corvette named the *Santa Rosa de Chacabuco,* whose own crew of diverse nationalities had mutinied against its revolutionary Argentinian masters off Chile and fled to Hawaii. Kamehameha had just purchased it for 6000 piculs (1 picul=133.3 lbs, meaning 400 tons) of sandalwood and many of its now compensated crew had scattered away on various ships to other Hawaiian islands.

Captain Bouchard quickly recognized that he could use the *Santa Rosa* as a consort ship. Forging documents as evidence, Captain Bouchard told Kamehameha that his purchase of this vessel was illegal and that he had been victimized by "pirates." He gave Kamehameha, through his "secretary," John Elliot d' Castro, the opportunity to be the first government in the world to "recognize" the newly independent government of Argentina. And he offered to buy back his new Argentinian government's stolen ship, the *Santa Rosa*, for the same amount that Kamehameha had paid for it. The aging Kamehameha, wanting to establish his own government as a leading actor in global events, agreed to Captain Bouchard's terms, signing a recognition document and assigning the powerful Chief Boki, Kalanimoku's younger brother, to accompany Bouchard in his travels on the *Santa Rosa* to the other islands to find and restore to service, or punish as he saw fit, the scattered crew.

When Captain Bouchard's *Santa Rosa*, with Boki and Don Francisco de Paula Marin aboard, reached Waimea on Kaua'i, they found Kamehameha's ship *Columbia* already anchored there under the command of Captain Jennings. Boki headed a delegation of Bouchard, Marin, and *Columbia's* first officer Peter Corney to an audience with King Kaumuali'i. Kaumuali'i informed them that indeed five members of the former crew of the *Santa Rosa* had recently resettled to Kaua'i. Four of these were living in Waimea village with commoners, and one, an Englishman called "Cap'n Griffiths," whom Bouchard alleged was the "pirates'" commander, was living under Kaumuali'i's "pu'uhonua" (sanctuary) in the Fort. After a brief polylingual conference, Boki announced to Kaumuali'i in Hawaiian that they expected him to have the four ordinary pirates arrested and returned to the *Santa Rosa* to be flogged and thereafter to take up continued service on its crew. But "Captain Griffiths" he was to execute for his leadership role in the act of piracy.

Kaumuali'i protested that Captain Griffiths was a subject of his personal sanctuary and said that he had spoken with him in English and thought that he could even be valuable to him as a foreign advisor. This angered Captain Bouchard who came up uncomfortably close to Kaumuali'i and, translated by Marin, threatened, "This man killed my ship's former officers and he lied to your King Kamehameha who was deceived into paying for the stolen ship. If he is not executed for this within six hours I will order the ships' cannons to commence firing upon both the village and the fort."[115]

Kaumuali'i, angered at this effrontery, responded, "for every shot from your cannons I will answer with twice twelve from ours. That's why we have cannons."

At this, Captain Bouchard and the others returned to their ships offshore. Kaumuali'i ordered his cannoneers at the fort to get the guns ready to fire, but within six hours he had the other four former crew members of the *Santa Rosa* arrested by his warriors and taken by canoe out to the ship. He gave much thought to what the consequences to Kaua'i might be if his cannon fire damaged or sunk Kamehameha's ship *Columbia*, or, much worse, killed or injured Kamehameha's Chief Boki or his friend and physician Marin.

Several sources say that in the morning Kaumuali'i decided to acquiesce to Bouchard's de-

---

[115] Mills 2002, p. 121, citing Neuman 1898, p. 26. See also Gast/Conrad, 1973, p. 65.

mand for Captain Griffiths' execution, that "after a short delay to grant the prisoner time to make his peace with his Maker, he was placed against the wall of the fort, shot and buried on the beach of Waimea."[116] But these reported circumstances are suspicious, especially the immediate burial on the beach. The mentioned delay, the fact that we are not told whether he was inside or outside the fort wall when shot...all quite strange. The witness Peter Corney's version is a bit different, saying that he was not shot at the wall, neither inside or outside...but just "on the beach."[117] And it appears that no one from the ships was ashore to witness this closely. They merely viewed events on the shore from the ships' distance.

My conjecture is that King Kaumuali'i staged a response to Captain Bouchard's threat which did not involve violation of the sanctuary he had granted the Englishman, whom he personally liked and considered valuable. He had someone else sacrificed instead...perhaps a kauwā or another ha' ole...likely someone already incarcerated for some other offense, or even scheduled for another execution in his fort's "dungeon." He had this substitute visibly dragged out onto Waimea Beach dressed very likely in Griffiths' clothes and the English-

[116] e.g. Mills 2002, p. 121, citing Neuman.

[117] Corney 1965, p. 216, and Bealer 1935, pp. 328-342.

man's tricorn hat. The reclothing could have been done during the reported "delay." This substitute "sacrifice" was then shot within the distant sight of those on the ships, and then immediately and visibly buried in order to eliminate possible examination of the body. This conjecture is consonant with other historical records of the Hawaiian Kings' response to foreigners' demands for retribution. Captain George Vancouver's demands from O'ahu Chief Kalanikūpule about the murder the month before of his first officer and astronomer on the *Daedalus* in 1793 elicited from Kalanikūpule a similar substitutive response.[118] Indeed Kaumuali'i may have heard about the ruse from Captain Vancouver himself, who suspected it.

I admit that I have found no hints about Captain Griffiths' subsequent fate. But I like to think that he lived to an old age on Kaua'i as did some (e.g. John Williams) of Kaumuali'i's other foreign advisors...maybe under a changed name. But the result of this incident had Captain Bouchard sailing happily away from Honolulu in October of 1818 with his ship *Argentina,* refitted and crewed by 290 men, including 50 natives from Hawaii, and his consort ship, the *Santa Rosa*, now captained by former first officer Peter Corney with its crew of 100 men, including 30 natives of Hawaii. They were bound for Argentina. And Kamehameha was

---

[118] Ibid, pp. 163-166.

well satisfied with Kaumuali'i's cooperation both commercial and civil.

THE DEATH OF KAMEHAMEHA—GREAT CHANGES:

On May 8, 1819, Kamehameha the Great died in his hale in the Kamakahonu settlement near the Ahuena Heiau at Kailua on Hawai'i island. He had been ill for a time, so that when the end was near, a number of people were present. One of these, a warrior chief and future governor of Kaua'i, Kaikio'ewa said to him on his death bed, "We are all here, your younger brothers, your chiefs, your foreigner (John Young called " 'Olohana"). Give us a word." "For what purpose?" asked Kamehameha. "As a saying for us (I hua na makou)" answered Kaikio'ewa. And Kamehameha answered with his last words, "Endless is the good that I have given you to enjoy (E 'oni wale no 'oukou i ku'u pono 'a'ole e pau)." That statement is a reflection of the fact that the last years of his rule were moderated in severity by his consideration of advice given to him by the many foreigners with whom he had come in contact and by the thoughts of his wives, primarily Ka'ahumanu and Keōpūolani. According with this was his instruction that his funeral rites should not, as they normally did for an ali'i nui, include any human sacrifices, because "all men are kapu" to his son and heir, Liholiho. But otherwise the traditional rites were observed. Liholiho went into a self-imposed exile in Kohala, as advised by the priest Hewahewa. The "heir's exile" was traditionally to last ten days while the Ali'i nui's body was cleaned and treated and the defilement created by death and its related activities was then removed through priestly ceremonies. Only after this completed treatment was the Ali'i nui's mana and full status able to be passed on to the returned heir.[119]

THE RITUAL CHAOS:

During this time there was by custom a "ritual chaos" among the people wherein ordinary relationships were disregarded...ali'i and maka'āinana were suddenly the same...and even the kapus ...all of them...were suspended. It was then the expected role of the new ruler to surmount the chaos and assert his power by reimposing the kapus and the traditional order of relationships. This period of chaos for Kamehameha extended more than the customary ten days. Ka'ahumanu and the other female chiefs went to the Ahuena Heiau, which was built in 1812 when Kamehameha moved his capital back to his home island as a "Hale o Lono

---

[119] Ibid, pp. 211-218.

heiau dedicated to the god Lono, and had meals prepared where they ate pork, bananas, coconuts and other fare that was ordinarily forbidden to them. And they mated sexually during the day ("ao"..."light") with strangers, even commoners, involving themselves in "kumakena aloha ali'i" (mourning for the ali'i by love), symbolically inviting the procreative forces of life to nullify the destructive force of death (symbolized by "pō," darkness) for the new ruler's sake. Ka'ahumanu inflicted cuts and burns on herself, and later had the English date "May 8, 1819" tattooed on her arm.[120] Others knocked out teeth.[121]

In its funerary treatment ("kapa lau" ceremony), Kamehameha's body was stripped of its flesh and the flesh taken out and committed to the ocean. The final disposition of his iwi was sacred and therefore very secretive. A special basket-like container called a "kā'ai," tightly woven of sennit, was fashioned.[122] The king's bones were encased in it. According to Dorothy Barrere, who drew upon

---

[120] By that time she already had tattoos on her left palm, her legs, and her tongue, See Kwiatkowski 1996, p.5.

[121] Silverman 1987, pp. 58-61, DauBach 1993, pp. 87-89 and also Sowel 2007, p. 85.

[122] Te Rangi Hiroa (Buck) 1957, pp. 576-577 il. Chapman 2004, pp. 57-61.

Kamakau, "the kā'ai was taken by Chief Ho'olulu to Kaloko in North Kona, to be deposited in a secret cave there under the direction of the High Chief Ulumaheihei Hoapili and Kamehameha's sacred wife Keōpūolani, who had been entrusted to hide the "iwi" (bones) "where no one would ever point them out." This they did so well that the bones have not been found to this day. Hawaiians say that "the morning star alone knows where Kamehameha's bones are guarded."[123]

LIHOLIHO SUCCEEDS—THE KAPUS ARE BROKEN:

After the ritual chaos ended, Kamehameha was succeeded by his son Liholiho, called also Kamehameha II, as planned, aided by "Kuhina nui" (Queen Regent) Ka'ahumanu and by Liholiho's mother, the most sacred Queen Keōpūolani. Great changes were immediately in the offing. These women high ali'i aspired to create a more modernized society, with a king whose primary responsibility was not to increase his mana, but to care for his people. And together they decided to do this by breaking the kapus. This essential underpinning of Hawaiian society they had come to

---

[123] See here Barrere 1994, p. 26, Cahill 1999, p. 124, and Kamakau 1992, pp. 212-215.

Liholiho (Kamehameha II), by John Hayter from Wikipedia.

think of as a hindrance to the development of the kind of society they envisioned for the future. Their first move was to violate, deliberately and openly, the old " 'ai kapu," the taboo preventing men and women from eating together. They arranged a banquet where the assembled chiefs witnessed Ka'ahumanu and Keōpūolani eating together with their now ruling advisee Liholiho.[124] Then they walked through assemblies of their subjects who were instructed not to prostrate themselves. The kapus, they announced, were over. There would be a new kind of rule in Hawaii.

It is important to understand that this discarding of the kapus was instigated by women...who had long been the most negatively effected by the kapu system. Also, that it was not, as is sometimes alleged, the consequence of the influence of Christian missionaries. The missionaries did not arrive in Hawaii until the next year, 1820. The most persuasive exterior influences conditioning the native decision to discard the kapus came from the foreign sea captains and the commercial traders. In November 1815 Ka'ahumanu admitted to Dr. George Anton Schaeffer that she had once eaten together with British seaman Thomas Manby and that "nothing happened" to her as a result, causing her to doubt that the kapus reflected the will of the gods. She asked Dr. Schaeffer if his wife ate together with him and with other men. When he answered that she did, Ka'ahumanu said that she had come to think that the 'ai kapu was not good.[125]

---

[124] Silverman 1987, p. 68.

[125] Croft 2012B, p. 144, see Manby 1929, pp. 11-23.

The inheritor of Kamehameha's Kūkā'ilimoku "Ki'i" (totem or idol), symbolizing the power of the war god, was Kekuaokalani, who was the son of Kamehameha's younger brother and a leading kahuna (priest). Kekuaokalani strongly opposed the overthrow of the kapus and organized a force of traditionalist chiefs and warriors to enforce the retention of the kapus. But Kamehameha's warrior chief Kalanimoku sided with Ka'ahumanu and Keōpūolani, and he led the loyalist forces to victory over Kekuaokalani and his warriors at the fierce Battle of Kuamo'o at a place called Lekeleke near Kailua in December of 1819. Both Kekuaokalani and his wife Manono were shot and killed in this battle.[126] Their bodies were left in the field and later buried under rock cairns with the other battle victims near a long ali'i sledding run ("holua") that has in modern times been intersected by a golf course.

It might seem strange that the very people instigating the overthrow of the kapus, and thus making a world-unprecedented sea change in their islands' culture, were those who had most benefitted from them...Ka'ahumanu, Keōpūolani, and Kalanimoku. But there was yet another unlikely advocate of change. Kamehameha's "Kahuna nui" (head priest) Hewahewa, himself a direct descendant of Pā'ao the initiator of the kapus and

---

[126] Kamakau 1992, p. 228, Warne 2008, p. 119.

Brook Kapūkuniahi Parker's 2016 painting of Hewahewa supervising the burning of the Ki'i (idols) in late 1819.

human sacrifice in the islands, realized that the overthrow of the kapus implied a refutation of the Hawaiian religion to which he had devoted his life. He could see that the times were rapidly evolving, and thus he was among the most forceful advocates of change. Soon after the initial breaking of the kapus he had declared that all religious observances at the heiaus were suspended, and he commenced the burning of all the "false idols" of which there were thousands on all the islands. The missionaries arrived some months later, and before too long Hewahewa, Ka'ahumanu and Keōpūolani all embraced Christianity. Later, in interviews with missionaries on O'ahu, he apologized for having represented false gods to the people and for sacrificing people to them.

In her 1968 article "The Overthrow of the Kapu System in Hawaii," Stephanie Seto Levin wrote: "With this suspension came the disenfranchisement of the orders of hereditary priests whose social and sacred functions reinforced and legitimized the existing political authority. Thus the abolition of the kapu system was to destroy most of the religious and supernatural foundations of the Hawaiian political structure." The popular reaction of the maka'āinana is well related in a version by later "Merrie Monarch" of Hawaii, David Kalākaua (1836-1891, whose wife, Queen consort Kapiolani was Kaumuali'i's granddaughter), who wrote about the abolition of the kapus and of the religious observances: " 'The *tabu* is broken! the *tabu* is broken!' passed from lip to lip, swelling louder and louder as it went, until it reached beyond the pavilion. There it was taken up in shouts by the multitude, and was soon wafted on the winds to the remotest corners of Kona. Feasts were at once provided, and men and women ate together indiscriminately. . . . At the conclusion of the royal feast a still greater surprise bewildered the people. 'We have made a bold beginning,' said Hewahewa to the king. . . 'but the gods and *heiaus* cannot survive the death of the *tabu.*' 'Then let them perish with it!' exclaimed Liholiho, now nerved to desperation at what he had done. 'If the gods can punish, we have done too much already to hope for grace. They can but kill, and we will test their powers by inviting the full measure of their wrath'."[127]

NO MORE "GOD KINGS," BUT WHAT ABOUT KAUMUALI'I?:

So by the time the first Christian missionaries arrived in the Hawaiian islands on March 20 of 1820,[128] the "Great King" Kamehameha was dead and the Hawaiian religion and its political underpinning kapu system had been deliberately abandoned by the succeeding ruler Liholiho and his powerful advisors Ka'ahumanu, Keōpūolani, Kalanimoku, and Hewahewa. After the Battle at Kuamo'o in December of 1819 they set about to install their own "anti-kapu" relatives into their governmental structure in every moku and ahupua'a on adjacent Maui, on Kaho'olawe, and on Lana'i, and Moloka'i, and on O'ahu. Where they absolutely ruled there were no more "God Kings" and their kapus and human sacrifices. But Ka'ahumanu and her cohort remembered well that Kamehameha had promised Kaumuali'i that he could continue to rule the relatively isolated Kaua'i "just as he had been until the end of his days." What did they know about Kaumuali'i's willingness to make the changes they were mak-

---

[127] See Rhodes from nps.gov .

[128] See Warne 2008, p. 113.

ing? As far as they knew, Kaumuali'i was now the "last God King" still observing the 'ai kapu, the prostration and other kapus, still practicing human sacrifice, still maintaining priests and all the former heiaus. And they reckoned he had every intention of ruling in this manner "until the end of his days."

We now know that Kaumuali'i broke the " 'ai kapu" and ate with his queens as early as the Fall of 1819 after hearing that Liholiho had begun the " 'ai noa" ("free eating") on Hawai'i island.[129] He was confident that he would face no divine retribution for doing this, nor for ordering his chiefs to have the people of Kaua'i make the change as well. He encountered no real opposition from his chiefs in doing this, as the word had already spread throughout all the islands about how this change of the 'ai kapu eating ritual had already taken place with only socially and interpersonally pleasant consequences in related but distant Tahiti, whence came the original kapu, and then, subsequently, on Hawai'i and the other islands.

Hewahewa's zealotry in abandoning the old religion, destroying what he called all the "false idols," and, most impactful of all, stripping the priests of their powerful social class status...their

---

[129] Kamakau 1992, p. 225 and see also Mills 2002, p. 131 for July 1820.

livelihoods, caused considerable opposition not only on Hawai'i and the other islands, but also on Kaua'i. Still, Kaumuali'i, a relative and admirer of Hewahewa, was resolute. At the end of the peaceful Makahiki season in February of 1820 he ordered the disenfranchisement of the priests, the destruction of heiaus, and the burning of the idols. As a recompense for not organizing armed opposition to him, Kaumuali'i granted tracts of land to several of the high priests. One of these was the aged kahuna Kū'ohu, who had once represented Kaumuali'i's parents among the first three Hawaiians to board Captain Cook's *Resolution* off Waimea in 1778. "I never opposed your mother," Kū'ohu told Kaumuali'i, "and I'll never oppose you." "But," he asked, "Do you mean to end the sacrificing?" " 'Ae, (yes)," was Kaumuali'i's answer. *Kaumuali'i's days as the "Last God King" were over…he had given it over himself.*

SON HUMEHUME RETURNS WITH THE MISSIONARIES:

Back in May of 1817 while Dr. George Anton Schaeffer was still resident on Kaua'i, Kaumuali'i had received the news from Captain William Heath Davis of the Boston ship *Eagle* that his son Humehume was alive and living with other Hawaiian young men in the American Board of Commissioners for Foreign Mission's (ABCFM) dormitory in Cornwall, Connecticut. Captain Heath read to

Kaumuali'i a letter Humehume had written him, informing Kaumuali'i about his life in the U.S. He had suffered many hardships, but had learned English well, played the viola well, and could even predict from astronomical charts a solar eclipse to be visible from Kaua'i in October of 1820, by which time he hoped to return to his "kulāiwi" ("native land"). He had served in the U.S. Marines and Navy and seen combat as a soldier and as a sailor. Severely wounded in a naval battle commanded by Captain Stephen Decatur, he had been hospitalized in France. After meeting Henry 'Opūkaha'ia (1792-1818), one of the first Hawaiian converts to Christianity, the Rev. Jedediah Morse, father of Samuel F. B. Morse, inventor of the telegraph and the Morse Code and the artist whose likeness of Humehume is given here below, had escorted him to visit the home of Yale University President Timothy Dwight. He was now called "George Prince Tamoree."[130] He had accepted the offer of education from the Foreign Mission school, but had stubbornly resisted the suggestion that he be baptized into the Christian faith.

The story of a father and son, separated for so long in such different cultures...and then reunited, is a very fascinating one. The ship *Thaddeus* Under Captain Andrew Blanchard, bringing the first delegation of Christian (Protestant) missionaries down

---

[130] See Warne 2008, pp. 41-100.

the Atlantic and around Cape Horn to Hawaii, reached Waimea, Kaua'i, after first leaving missionaries on Hawai'i island and on O'ahu, on May 3, 1820. Humehume had, during the short stay at Kailua on Hawai'i island, met and married in the traditional Hawaiian way Betty Davis (called in Hawaiian "Pake"), the daughter of Kamehameha's poisoned English advisor Isaac Davis, who had in 1810 lost his life by saving that of Kaumuali'i.

The actual father-and-son reunion took place in the stone house Kaumuali'i called, as he had previous personal residences, "Papa'ena'ena," which had been constructed for him by Dr. George Anton Schaeffer three years before. When Humehume entered, accompanied by missionaries Samuel Ruggles and Samuel Whitney, Kaumuali'i and his Queen Kekaiha'akulou were sitting on a European-style sofa. There were many Hawaiians already gathered there, standing very close together along the inner walls and also looking in the windows from the outside. Kaumuali'i, dressed in his finest cloak and cap, got up, hugged his son in his arms and pressed his nose to his son's in the "honi" way, sharing a breath with him. Both were unable to speak for some time. The missionaries reported that the scene was "truly affecting."[131]

---

[131] Ibid, p. 132-135, also Soboleski 2003, p. 41.

Brook Kapūkuniahi Parker's 2017 painting of the "Father and Son Reunion."[132]

---

[132] See Parker in the Biblio for an identification of the people in the painting.

A NEW RIVALRY, AS IN DAYS PAST:

At their reunion Kaumuali'i draped on his son Humehume's shoulders a magnificent long feathered 'ahu'ula cape, the visible symbol of an ali'i, and appointed him chief of the Waimea District (ahupua'a) in which he, the king of all Kaua'i and Ni'ihau, lived. This symbolic act brought about a "mana rivalry" for his own succession between his first-born son Humehume and his sacred-wife-born son Keali'iahonui. Both young men, although they had grown up in very different ways and in very different places, expected to succeed their father as king of Kaua'i. Humehume had gained even more worldly experience and skills than Kaumuali'i could have foreseen when he sent him away at the age of four to be educated in New England...his succession could only be seen as advantageous. But Keali'iahonui was the legitimate heir traditionally...his "mana" more pure by definition of having both father and mother being ali'i siblings. And the chiefs and the wives...especially Kekaiha'akulou and his mother Kapua'amohu...clearly favored Keali'iahonui. The rivalry developed quickly, reminding Kaumuali'i of his own rivalry twenty-five years before with his own half-brother Keawe. Who would prevail?

FATHER AND SON, BUT NOT ALL THE SAME:

Kaumuali'i made the missionaries, Samuel Whitney and Samuel Ruggles and their wives, who had come to Hawaii on the *Thaddeus* with his son, feel welcome, having another stone house constructed for both of their families adjacent to his own. But in the next months his son Humehume, trying to adopt Hawaiian customs, irritated his missionary sponsors by maintaining his refusal to be baptized as a Christian, while his father Kaumuali'i himself now became increasingly amenable to the missionaries' Christian instruction, praising often their "one all-powerful God" doctrine. He learned about Jesus and about how those who tried in their lives to live in love and tolerance as he had could expect eternal reward in God's presence in heaven. He was even more than characteristically curious about Christianity, and frequently engaged the missionaries in direct discussions...and he came even to seek their advice.

In July of 1820 Humehume wrote a letter to Herman Daggett, his former instructor at the Foreign Mission School in Cornwall, Connecticut, telling him, in part: "...I shall not write many particulars, as I shall send you my journal. I can only write a few lines to let you know that I have not forgotten you. You are, Sir, very dear to me. I often take great pleasure in meditating on what you have taught me, in former days; and hope, dear friend, that you will have the pleasure of hearing the virtue of your words to me. *You cannot but rejoice to hear that my father has demolished his idols* (Italics mine, author). The event took place before my arrival here (he arrived in May 3, 1820). How astonished were all at this information! They seem to think that the Governor of the universe had surely begun to display his mighty power. Now it is peace and harmony; *and the female, who was before trodden beneath, is now on the same footing. Now the man and wife, son and daughter, eat and drink in the same social band* (Italics mine, author). It is very pleasing to me…P.S. I send with this letter a particular family idol of my father."[133] I think it interesting that Humehume refers to the Christian God he has been learning about for five years as the "Governor of the universe." And I conjecture that the "particular family idol of my father" is a carved "ki'i 'aumakua" (family god used in worship) of a "mo'o," the lizard " 'aumakua" of Kaumuali'i's genealogical line.

In that same month, Kaumuali'i himself wrote to thank the American Board of Commissioners for Foreign Missions' (ABCFM) secretary, Samuel Worcester, for the Bible he had been given: "Dear Friend, I wish to write a few lines to thank you for the good book you was so kind as to send by my

---

[133] Warne 2008, p. 140.

son. I think it is a good book. One that God gave us to read. I hope my people will soon read this and all other good books. *I believe that my idols are good for nothing. My gods I have hove away. They are no good. They fool me and they do me no good. I give them coconuts, plaintains, hogs and many good things and they fool me at last. Now I throw them all away. I have none now. When your good people learn me I worship your God* (Italics mine, author). I feel glad you good people come here to help us...I thank all American people. I feel good to see you good folks here. Suppose you come I take good care of them. I hope you take good care of my people in your country. Suppose you do I feel glad. I must close. Accept this from your friend, King Tamoree."[134]

As Kaumuali'i became more and more agreeable with the Christian values espoused by the missionaries Samuel Whitney and Samuel Ruggles, Humehume continued to refuse baptism. He also began to drink rum and other alcoholic drinks to excess, causing him troubles and admonishments, whereas his father Kaumuali'i eschewed the "ha'ole" (white man's) alcohol, preferring the native " 'awa," even though it made his skin appear "scaly" to foreign observers. Humehume's wife Betty gave birth to a baby boy in December, 1820, but the health of both mother and son was

---

[134] Ibid, p. 141.

persistently precarious, causing them serious concerns.

THE HULA AND SEXUAL RELATIONS:

In the next year the missionary couples Whitney and Ruggles were often invited by Kaumuali'i, his queens, and his chiefs to Hawaiian traditional events and rituals. Their reaction to these events and rituals were the subject of much discussion between the people of the native Hawaiian culture and the American Protestant Christian world. Consider Mercy Whitney's reaction, from her journal entry of January 22, 1821 to the Hula: "A few days since Mr. W. and myself were going to the Kings; when about half way we were informed that the King and Queen were at the hula hula (native dance). Curiosity had many times prompted me to go and witness this scene of their diversions, but not being able to speak the language sufficiently to convince them of their folly, I had doubted the propriety of it, but being then near the place, we concluded to go. They were in a large yard on the bank of the sea, fenced off for that purpose. A great number of them were there collected and several rows formed consisting of men, women, and children: these were placed a sufficient distance from each other for gestures which are of the most immodest kind, and which constitute the greater part of their diversion. The head and ankles were wreathed with grass and flowers; the body naked except a strip of cloth about the loins, usually of different colours. They all sing or make noise. The voice never varies from the key note. Here they assemble and spend two or three hours morning and evening. If any absent themselves without special leave from the King, they are liable to a severe punishment. In viewing the faithfulness of these poor creatures to their heathen Master I was led to reflect upon the inconstancy of many of the professed followers of Jesus. I thought to myself were Christians but as faithful to their Divine Lord, how much honor might they reflect upon his blessed character."[135]

Here I conjecture a dialogue based on attitudes elsewise reflected in their relationship. It involves Samuel Whitney asking Kaumuali'i in English about the Hula dancing. Kaumuali'i surely tried to explain to him that: "The Hula is a way in which we express our gratitude for the abundance and the beauty of our home, Kaua'i. The dance's motions and gestures symbolize elements of nature: the sea, the mountains, the fields, the forests, the rivers… for which we are grateful and thus dance to give thanks."

"But we think the motions and the gestures are sinful because they seem to represent intimate hu-

---

[135] Ibid, pp. 134-135.

man relations. The dancers show their nakedness and seem to encourage people to fornication," said Whitney.

"It is true that we are also grateful for each other, Brother Samuel, and our Hula shows this," continued Kaumuali'i. "We share the dance with each other just as we share our lives with each other. We have always done this. It is a valued tradition with us. It makes us feel we are one… and we share this feeling together. And besides, we don't feel that sharing intimate human relations is bad. To us, these relations are a good thing that we share. And we dance to express our gratitude for that too."

But Samuel Whitney persisted to explain: "Our religion teaches us that these human relations are for making babies as part of a marriage held sacred in the eyes of our Lord. All other sex is sinful fornication which will lead to damnation. That is why Brother Samuel Ruggles and I refuse when your men offer their wives to us for our sexual gratification. We think this to be sinful and that we would go to Hell if we shared such intimacy with your women outside of our marriages."[136]

"We have much to learn, Brother Samuel," said Kaumuali'i. "But I assure you that our Hula and

---

[136] Ibid, p. 130.

the intimacy we share with each other are good things. I can't believe that your all-knowing God Jehovah does not know this."

Samuel Whitney shook his head, then, out of curiosity, asked Kaumuali'i about his many wives. "Have you ever shared any of your wives with others?"

"Yes," answered Kaumuali'i. "I have shared some of my wives with others when I thought it helpful to me. I shared Kapua'amohu with others to help me overcome my brother Keawe and become Ali'i nui. I shared Kekaiha'akulou with Kamaholelani so that he would become my messenger to Kamehameha. And I have shared others too. Kamehameha also did this. Once he gave a wife to Kamaholelani."[137]

"Do you not have one wife that you love more than the others and that you would therefore not share?" asked Whitney.

"No, Brother Samuel," Kaumuali'i answered. "I feel strong aloha for all my wives, but being jealous about them is not good. It's what we would call a sin."

---

[137] Ibid, p. 111.

"Have any of them that you offered to another ever refused to lie with that other?" asked Whitney.

"No," answered Kaumuali'i. "None have refused."

A SAD TIME FOR KAUMUALI'I:

In February of 1821, Kaumuali'i's fifteen-year-old son Kahekili by his wife and Queen Namahana lost his appetite and would not eat. He suffered swelling and pain in his abdomen and became fevered. After a week of this, he died, despite the best efforts of the priests and the medical advice of the missionaries and other foreigners. Samuel Whitney wrote that rumors spread that someone had prayed young Kahekili to death. Queen Kekaiha'akulou, who was very fond of Kahekili, reportedly sent her bodyguards to kill a priest that she suspected of doing this. But this priest fled and appealed to Kaumuali'i's sister Kapi'olani, who saved his life by gaining Kaumuali'i's intercession in the matter.

I here conceive another imagined dialogue that envisions Samuel Whitney asking Kaumuali'i about his son Kahekili's death, asking him if someone might have prayed him to death.

"I was praying every day that he would be well," answered Kaumuali'i, "And no one else has prayer so powerful as to overcome this."

Whitney likely offered his consolation, saying, "We believe that our Lord's need for your son was greater than our wish that he keep living here. He was a good young man, and we like to think that he will now be living in Heaven."

"I am now praying that that is true," said Kaumuali'i. "I remember him as a good keiki. He was fearless. Once when he was only nine of your years old he climbed to the top of the rigging on the Russian ship *Otkrytie* when his older brother dared him to do so. And he was smart. He quickly learned to speak and understand Russian from his kumu (teacher), the ha'ole Tarakanov. I told Kepa (Dr. George Anton Schaeffer, LBC) that he would one day meet the Russian Tsar. But now, auwē (alas), he won't."

"Do you want us to say a blessing at his funeral?" asked Whitney.

"You can say a blessing, Brother Whitney," said Kaumuali'i, "but we will be giving him our kind of funeral. We will give his flesh to the sea, and his iwi will be kept by his mother, my Queen Namahana, perhaps even in a kā'ai (woven torso-shaped sennit casket). Such is Namahana's wish."[138]

KAUMUALI'I IS TESTED:

In July of 1821, Chiefess Kalakua, a sister of Ka'ahumanu's who had been a consort of Kamehameha's, sailed with a group of her retainers to Kaua'i on the New York merchant schooner *Tartar*.[139] Captain Benjamin Morrel anchored the ship off Waimea and sent crew members ashore to announce Chiefess Kalakua's presence. She was requesting an audience with King Kaumuali'i. Kaumuali'i, realizing her importance, decided to give her a truly royal visit to his capital. He and Queen Kekaiha'akulou met her at the shore, he in his feather regalia, embracing her with "honi" (the joining of noses by which to share a breath). Kaumuali'i told Kalakua that he had temporarily vacated his grand new stone house so that she might reside there during her stay on Kaua'i. Kalakua was most pleased with this reception, but immediately informed Kaumuali'i that she wanted to eat together with him and his queens, and that she expected that pork would be on the menu…

---

[138] See Te Tangi Hiroa (Sir Peter Buck) 2003, pp. 575-577.

[139] TenBruggencate 2015, p. 30.

thus practicing the new " 'ai noa" (free eating) perhaps not yet sanctioned on Kaua'i.

Kaumuali'i understood that this was a kind of test, likely planned by Liholiho and Ka'ahumanu, to see if he was amenable to the new "no kapu" lifestyle they had already spread throughout the other Hawai'ian islands. He would show her that on Kaua'i the 'ai kapu was already broken. So he ordered a crew of twenty people (both men AND women) to slaughter and cook pigs, dogs, and chickens for a banquet which was served on the best Ni'ihau makaloa mats in front of his Papa-ena-ena residence overlooking the Waimea River's flow into the ocean. The missionaries and their wives, Mercy Whitney and Nancy Ruggles, were also in attendance.

But Kaumuali'i did not completely pass the "test" that Chiefess Kalakua's visit presented to him. In their conversation she gave her opinion that he had not sufficiently restructured Kaua'i's control of the land. The chiefs were still all the same chiefs...none had been replaced as they had in the rest of the realm. She proposed to help him select new chiefs, chiefs famliar with the way things were now being done on the other islands, chiefs who were, he understood, closer related members of the Kamehameha line. This angered Kaumuali'i. He was proud, he said, of Kaua'i "the way it is" and listed for Kalakua all the prominent

Hawaiians from other islands who had decided in the past to make their residence there because of his rule, even kinder and more just, he said, than Kamehameha's vaunted "Kānāwai Māmalohoe" ("Law of the Splintered Paddle"... meaning justice and protection from harm for all, ali'i and maka'āinana alike).[140] "Maika'i Kaua'i." he said, "Hemolele i ka Mālie" ("Beautiful is Kaua'i—Perfect in the calm").[141]

LIHOLIHO COMES TO KAUA'I:

Later in the summer of 1821, Liholiho, sailed from the big island of Hawai'i to Honolulu with a party of about thirty of his retinue. After drinking there with friends, he ordered that they all go on a fishing trip, which he then extended to include a crossing of the Ka'ie'ie Waho Channel so that he could visit Kaumuali'i in Kaua'i. Despite serious difficulties with the currents, Liholiho forced his company to stay the course, arriving two long days later at Waimea. His sudden unannounced presence there with only a small retinue of men and women gave an easy opportunity, should he have wanted it, for Kaumuali'i to order their discreet

---

[140] See Hawaii Legal Authority site.

[141] These are the words to a well-known Hawaiian song.

demise. But instead he offered to turn over to Liholiho all his lands, forts, ships, guns, and people immediately. Liholiho politically assured him that such was not his desire, saying, "I did not come to dispossess you. Keep your country and take care of it as before." Instead he asked Kaumuali'i for a complete tour of the island for him and his retinue, and Kaumuali'i agreed, knowing that such an "official tour" would demand considerable resources and take a month or more. As he arranged this tour as rapidly as he could, he asked his son Humehume to come along. As it turned out, the tour, involving about a hundred people, took 42 days.

THE KAPUS ARE BROKEN ON KAUA'I FOR ALL TO SEE:

The announced purpose of Liholiho's required tour was to assure himself that ALL of Kaua'i be shown that King Kaumuali'i—his sons, his queens, and his chiefs, all acceded to the new no-kapu lifestyle presented by Hawaii's new "Ali'i nui," himself...that the credit for it was his. All the tour's feasts were " 'ai noa" ("free eating," meaning men and women together). No prostration kapu was required. No kapu-enforcing mū were in evidence at all. The people were fed and entertained by horseback riding and athletic exhibitions and by music and dances, sports and games. In every ahupua'a Kaumuali'i introduced Liholiho and the new no-kapu lifestyle to his chiefs, konohiki, and even the maka'āinana. It was a new life for all. Yet Liholiho had another less obvious purpose. He was looking at every ahupua'a and moku as places to install his own chiefs.

KA'AHUMANU AND KALANIMOKU COME TO KAUA'I TOO:

While Liholiho's tour of Kaua'i was going on, Kaumuali'i sent his brig *Becket*, that he had purchased seven months before, to find Ka'ahumanu on either O'ahu or Hawai'i to inform her of Liholiho's whereabouts and status. When Ka'ahumanu and Kalanimoku were informed of this, they gathered together crew and staff, and Liholiho's five wives, and took to the sea in the historic ship *Ha'aheo o Hawai'i* ("The Pride of Hawai'i"). This ship was constructed for the wealthy magnate George Crowninshield, Jr. (1766-1817) and christened *Cleopatra's Barge* in Salem, Massachusetts, in 1816.[142] It was the first luxury yacht built in the United States, and it was so extravagantly appointed as to draw large crowds wherever it appeared.

---

[142] See http://en.wikipedia.org/wiki/Cleopatras_Barge. The Captain here was likely Alexander Adams, and not Jean Baptiste Rives or Naihekukui, both of whom also have fascinating Wikipedia entries.

Queen Ka'ahumanu (1768-June 5, 1832) in image by J. J. Williams after portrait by Louis Choris in 1816, from Wikipedia. Notice that in this image we see no tattoos (see Biblio. under "Tattoos")

Liholiho had purchased it in 1820 after Crowninshield's death by selling five hundred tons of sandalwood, worth a sum equivalent to a million of today's U. S. dollars...and he renamed the ship.

When the grand *Ha'aheo o Hawai'i* appeared off Waimea just as Kaumuali'i's tour of Kaua'i for Liholiho had ended, it caused a sensation. Hundreds of canoes were paddled out to surround and view it. Liholiho was paddled out to it so that he could assure Regent Ka'ahumanu, Kalanimoku, and his own five wives, that he was all right. He also told them, much to the women's consternation, that he had decided during his tour of Kaua'i to give his fifth wife, Kekauluohi, a niece of Ka'ahumanu's, to his friend, Chief Kana'ina, who had advocated his immediate taking over of Kaua'i from Kaumuali'i...this apparently as a kind of recompense for his postponement of any such action. But, to fill Kekauluohi's place in his family of wives, he said that he would take Kaumuali'i's Queen Kekaiha'akulou to be his fifth wife.[143] Ka'ahumanu was initially quite displeased by this "new wife" of Liholiho's, thinking the exchange to be a slighting in mana of her niece Kekauluohi. But a kahuna there reminded her that Kekaiha'akulou was, through her father, Chief Haupu, a cousin of Ka'ahumanu's with a powerful mana of her own.

A few hours later, after a short sailing race alongside Kaumuali'i's *Becket*,[144] Liholiho invited Kaumuali'i, and only Kaumuali'i (i.e. not Hume-

---

[143] Kamakau 2002, p. 253.

[144] See Joesting 1984, p. 93.

hume and not Kekaiha'akulou), to tour his *Ha'aheo o Hawai'i*. Kaumuali'i went aboard, and after he was served a few alcoholic drinks he felt he could not refuse, he noticed that Liholiho had left the reception compartment, shutting and locking the door, and that he had ordered the ship to sail away. Kaumuali'i had been kidnapped. Liholiho, Ka'ahumanu and Kalanimoku took him without announcement or explanation to anyone to O'ahu where Liholiho had a compound at Waikīkī.

A MARRIAGE PROPOSAL?

At Liholiho's compound, Kaumuali'i was given a quite surprising, but quite clever, ultimatum by Regent Ka'ahumanu. He could marry her and enjoy henceforth all the largesse such a position would entail...and peace would continue to reign. Or he could refuse and she would have him killed...causing doubtless disorder and destruction to his people on Kaua'i and Ni'ihau. She would, if he agreed to the marriage, be a partner in rule with the two extant "ali'i nui" in the islands...her foster son Liholiho and her "husband" Kaumuali'i. No one, she said, could possibly oppose this trio. Kaumuali'i didn't have to think a long time about it. Two weeks later, on October 9, 1821, a traditional Hawaiian ceremony of marriage took place between Kaumuali'i, Ali'i nui of Kaua'i and Ni'ihau, and Ka'ahumanu, widow of Kamehameha and regent of the other Hawaiian islands with Liholiho. After chants and rituals, they lay together on a platform and servants covered them with a kapa spread. They were thereafter husband and wife. And Kaumuali'i never attempted to escape the bonds of this matrimony, not even during a trip he made with Ka'ahumanu back to Kaua'i months later. Though missionary Charles Stewart wrote that the marriage bond was not a "silken cord," Ka'ahumanu took pride in her acquisition of Kaumuali'i as a husband and she liked to "show him off." He was a tall, handsome man, slenderer than Kamehameha had been, but muscular. His nose and face was said to resemble that of the white men, and he dressed in western gentlemen's clothes, as opposed to Liholiho, who usually appeared in his native "malo" (loincloth), and he carried also a gold pocket watch.

As part of the abduction scheme, Ka'ahumanu appointed her brother Kahekili Ke'eaumoku to be governor of Kaua'i in Kaumuali'i's stead. This Kahekili Ke'eaumoku, and his successors, Kalanimoku's nephew Kāhalai'a and Kamehameha's warrior nephew Kaikio'ewa, governed Kaua'i and Ni'ihau (and including uninhabited Lehua and more distant Nihoa) as Ka'ahumanu instructed them.. She and Liholiho desired to replace with their own cronies and relatives most of the former ali'i 'ai moku (district chiefs) and the ahupua'a konohiki to collect the taxes still required of the now religionless maka'āinana. In this way, Ka'ahumanu and her proxies could control ALL the land in the islands as they wished. Only Kalanimoku resisted the immediate replacement of Kaua'i's chiefs in deference to Kaumuali'i's strong desire that they should remain in place.

QUEEN KEKAIHA'AKULOU BECOMES DEBORAH KAPULE:

Kaua'i Queen Kekaiha'akulou was one of the first people of Kaua'i to accept baptism into the Christian faith taught by the missionaries. She took the Christian name "Deborah Kapule" (meaning "Deborah the Prayer"). She was stunned when, on Kaumuali'i's tour of Kaua'i with him, the new "Ali'i nui" Liholiho requested that Kaumuali'i give her up to him as a replacement for his fifth wife. When Kaumuali'i agreed to this request, she could not believe it. She fell into deep despair. But only days later Liholiho left her on Kaua'i when he sailed away with the abducted Kaumuali'i on his grand ship. There had been no further announcement and no ceremony of marriage. Then in another three weeks she got the news that Kaumuali'i had married the Regent Ka'ahumanu and intended to stay indefinitely with her wherever she went. She talked about this with her sister queens, with her father, the Chief Haupu (also called Kaiawa), and with the missionaries. When she discussed the matter with her sister queen Kapua'amohu, she got a most interesting suggestion...that since she now no longer had a husband, she should marry Kapua'amohu's son, Keali'iahonui, Kaumuali'i's expected heir and successor. Keali'iahonui, only a few years younger than Kapule (Kekaiha'akulou), readily agreed to this proposal when his mother told him of it, and the couple was then formally married. Thus occurred another example of the ever-transpiring kinship, power, and rivalry links of the ali'i class.

BUT KA'AHUMANU MARRIES THE SON TOO:

Humehume was incensed at this union, since it gave ever more credibility to his younger brother Keali'iahonui's claim to succeed their father as "Ali'i nui," or even as "Ali'i aimoku" under Liholiho. But Humehume's distress at the marriage was short-lived, because Keali'iahonui joined a group to visit his father Kaumuali'i on O'ahu, and Ka'ahumanu allowed this group to see him. She was impressed herself with Keali'iahonui's tall appearance and confident bearing, and she quickly understood that he represented a potential threat to her control over Kaua'i. So she had him seized and put the marriage ultimatum to him too. They were formally married in the Spring of 1822.

Ka'ahumanu paraded through Honolulu in a warrior-drawn carriage squeezed between her new husbands Kaumuali'i and his son Keali'iahonui.

DEBORAH KAPULE'S LATER LIFE:

On Kaua'i, Kapule was once again husbandless, but she would not remain so. In 1824 she married Simeona Kaiu, a half-brother of Kaumuali'i's, being, I conjecture, a son of Kaumuali'i's father Ka'eo with a maka'āinana woman. Kapule and Simeona Kaiu moved from Waimea to Wailua in 1835 where they lived in a house at the place where travelers forded the Wailua River on their way north or south along the eastern coast. Simeona spoke English well (having had some of the same instructors as Kaumuali'i) and became a dynamic preacher who once traveled away to the Marquesas Islands on a Christian mission, and with him Kapule had a son they named Josiah Kaumuali'i Kaiu. Kapule and Kaiu started a church in Wailua, but she lost interest in it after he suddenly died in 1836. She continued to manage their house as an inn for travelers and operated several fish ponds where sea fish were gradually transferred to fresh water ponds to be fattened for market. By 1840 she had taken up relations with a Wailua resident, Oliver Chapin, whose wife Nihinu, said to be "a cripple," was a daughter of Kaumuali'i by Naluahi. Her scandalous relationship with Chapin caused the church she had found-ed to excommunicate her, but, by 1850, she had been restored to its membership. When her son Josiah died in 1854 she was heart-broken and died on 26 August, 1855.[145]

HUMEHUME OPPOSES KA'AHUMANU'S REGIME IN KAUA'I:

"George Prince Tamoree," (Humehume) in an 1816 painting by telegraph inventor Samuel F. B. Morse (1791-1872), from Wikipedia.

---

[145] Joesting 1987, pp. 113-118, Soboleski 2003, pp. 41-45.

In February, 1822, Humehume's and Betty Davis's baby boy became sick and died. Unlike the Hawaiian ali'i ritual given to Kaumuali'i's son Kahekili only a year before, an elaborate funeral had the baby buried in the Christian manner with a blessing by the missionaries inside Waimea's Fort Elizaveta on what had once been the holy ground of the Pā'ula'ula o Hipo Heiau, showing that the baby had been considered an "ali'i." The child's body may have been located but not disturbed during a archeological "dig" done in the Fort in 1993.[146] Humehume began thereafter to show his dissatisfaction with how Ka'ahumanu's chosen Governor, Kahekili Ke'eaumoku, and his successor, Kalanimoku's nephew Kāhalai'a, ran Kaua'i.

THE PASSING OF A CHRISTIAN NAMED HARRIET: KEŌPŪOLANI

In mid-September, 1823, Ka'ahumanu and her two husbands traveled to Lahaina, Mau'i, to visit the Sacred Queen Keōpūolani, who was ill and close to death. Liholiho and Kalanimoku came there also. Keōpūolani, who had accepted Christianity and serenely advocated it to the others, had decided as she learned from the missionaries to

---

[146] On this and other possible Fort burials, see Mills 2002, pp. 215, 224.

oppose the polygamy practiced by the ali'i. Since she had married both Kalanimoku and Hoapili Ulumaheihei after the death of Kamehameha and the overthrow of the old kapus, she now resolutely

Sacred Queen Keōpūolani (1778-Sept. 16, 1823), image from Wikipedia.

but sadly informed Kalanimoku that he could no longer be her husband because she and Hoapili would be husband and wife only to each other. But when she saw Kalanimoku at her bedside there, she clearly remembered that he, her ex-husband, the warriors' warrior and "Iron Cable," had been baptized together with his brother Boki into the Catholic Christian faith on the French ship *Uranie* with Ka'ahumanu and Liholiho as witnesses as early as 1819, taking as his "Christian name" "Guillaumé" (the French for "William" as of his English nickname "Billy Pitt"). She extended her hand to Kalanimoku and told him, "I love Jesus Christ. I have given myself to him to be his." Then, minutes before her death, she was baptized and given the Christian name of Harriet in honor of missionary C. S. Stewart's wife. All the visitors were deeply impressed also with the Christian funeral service and the burial procession Keōpūolani was given. The Ali'i then shared the task with the great numbers of grieving makā'ainana hauling large rocks to make a stone funeral cairn for Keōpūolani at the Mokuhinia Pond's ali'i interment site in Lahaina called "Moku'ula."[147]

At this time, Kaumauli'i told Ka'ahumanu that if he were to die, he did not want his body to be defleshed and his "iwi" (bones) wrapped in kapa (bark cloth) and placed alongside anyone's sleeping mat. This was a reference to the fact that Ka'ahumanu kept the bones of her father, Ke'eaumoku, close by her at all times so as to in-

---

[147] See Klieger 1998, p. 33.

crease her mana and that of her place.[148] And he did not want his iwi put into a kā'ai and hidden in some cave like some notable of his ali'i ancestors had been.[149] Instead, he told Ka'ahumanu, he wanted to be buried whole in a coffin "like the Christians are," and he wanted that coffin to be buried "at Keōpūolani's feet." He told her that he and Keōpūolani had already agreed that they "would rise up to God in Heaven together when Jesus returns and the great resurrection takes place."[150]

LIHOLIHO SAILS TO ENGLAND:

While he was at Keōpūolani's funeral, the capricious Liholiho met English Captain Valentine Starbuck of the ship *L'Aigle*, who was preparing to sail to the British Isles. Captain Starbuck suggested that Liholiho sail with him to London, so that he could "meet King George (i.e. George IV) face-to-face and see how he ruled England." Liholiho precipitously announced that he would do just that. He formally designated his younger brother Kauikeaouli, then just nine years old, to be his successor in the event that he did not return, and sailed on the *L'Aigle* with his favorite wife,

---

[148] Silverman 1987, p. 43.

[149] Chapman 2004, pp. 58-61.

[150] Zambucka 1999, p. 78 and 81.

Kamāmalu and his friends Boki and Kuini Liliha, for England. This essentially left Regent Ka'ahumanu in sole command of the Kingdom.

THE SHIP *HA'AHEO O HAWAI'I* IS LOST:

Ka'ahumanu and Kalanimoku sent the ship *Ha'aheo o Hawai'i* to Kaua'i to ascertain the loyalty of some of Kaumuali'i's chiefs to his son Humehume, who, it was rumored, was preparing an armed rebellion against them. It is unclear just who was in command of the ship, since the known captains of it—Alexander Adams, Naihekukui, and Jean Baptiste Rives—were attested to be elsewhere. Naihekukui, known also as "Captain Jack," and Rives were both with Liholiho and his party in London. And just why the ship was crossing Hanalei Bay on the remote north coast of Kaua'i is also unclear. But, on April 6, 1824, the ship ran aground on a shallow reef near the entry into the bay of Wai'oli Stream and slumped over onto its side. Those aboard were easily able to get to shore and there was no reported loss of life or serious injury.

In a couple of weeks Kaumuali'i's Chief of Waipouli, Kia'imakani, called "The Blind" ("Makapō") because of his poor vision, organized a large force of native men to go to

Hanalei to right the ship. They used their bare hands to make three enormous ropes by braiding the inner bark of the hau tree, common along Hawaii's coasts and streams. They then tied the ropes to the ship's main mast, planning to roll it across the reef back into an upright position. Kia'imakani led them in a rhythmic chant to Lono as they then pulled with all their mass might on the ropes. Samuel Whitney estimated their number at more than a thousand. It was the greatest application of human muscle power he had ever witnessed. And the ship was indeed returned to an upright position, but only too briefly. The mast snapped off at the deck and all the rigging fell into the sea as the grand ship rolled back onto its side.

The workers knew that another attempt should be made. But they commenced salvage work, not only to carry off things of value in an effort at preservation, but also to lighten the ship so that it might be rolled back upright more easily. This work was prolonged and many of the men returned to their homes. There they were told that their King, Kaumuali'i, was gravely ill and dying in Honolulu. Dispirited, they did not return to make further efforts to right the ship. It was left to be broken up by the surf, and in a month or two there was none of it visible above the surf.[151]

KAUMUALI'I PASSES AWAY WITH A CHRISTIAN BLESSING:

In May of 1824, word came to Humehume from O'ahu that his father Kaumuali'i had been stricken with a serious lung condition called pleurisy and was gravely ill. Humehume decided to remain in Wahiawa village on Kaua'i, where he and Betty had taken up residence after the death of their baby son, and await further communication from O'ahu. He later regretted this decision. His father, Kaumuali'i, Ali'i nui of Kaua'i and Ni'ihau, died in Ka'ahumanu's Honolulu residence on Wednesday May 26, 1824, at nine o'clock in the morning, after welcoming a bedside blessing by the Christian missionaries William Ellis and C. S. Stewart and attended by Ka'ahumanu, Kalanimoku, and Keali'iahonui. He was not yet 44 years old (his father had died at 35, his mother at 44). Though he was

---

[151] See http://en.wikipedia.org/wiki/Cleopatras_Barge. Also Mills 2003, p. 143. The effort to find the sunken ship in the late 1990s by the Smithsonian Institution's Paul Forsythe Johnston and especially Captain Rick Rogers is fascinating.

likely amenable to it, he was never baptized as a Christian.

As Kaumuali'i was in his last minutes of life, Kalanimoku leaned over him and asked him to name his heir. "After your death, who is to be your successor?" he asked. Kaumuali'i looked at Ka'ahumanu and replied "our son." By this those at his deathbed understood that he had named "Liholiho" as his successor, as he had once promised Kamehameha. Then Kalanimoku asked: "What about the lands of Kaua'i? Who will have the lands?" Kaumuali'i said, "Let the lands be as they are; those chiefs who have lands are to hold them; those who have no lands are to get none."[152]

Humehume received the news of Kaumuali'i's death on Friday, May 28, 1824, so that, despite his best effort, he did not make it to the funeral, which took place in Honolulu that same day. Crowds of makā'ainana had viewed Kaumuali'i's cloaked and draped body on a pink velvet settee through Ka'ahumanu's residence window. There was then a Christian service outside the residence and a procession of multitudes of people in Honolulu, bearing Kaumuali'i's coffin to the harbor, from where Ka'ahumanu and Keali'iahonui transported it to Lahaina, Maui. There it was interred beside

---

[152] Kamakau 1992, pp. 265-266, Wichman 2003, pp. 110-111.

Author Lee B. Croft places a small stone from Kaua'i's "Russian Fort" onto the base of Kaumuali'i's grave in Lahaina, Maui. The stone was removed later the same day by the cemetery caretakers. 2015 Photo by Lesley Hoyt Croft.

Keōpūolani's grave at Moku'ula, the stonework of which Kaumuali'i had himself helped construct the year before.

On Kaua'i there was a great popular outpouring of grief and a time of "ritual chaos" in order to commemorate Kaumuali'i's passing. According to Kamakau: "the men blackened their thighs (pa'ele kākau)...see "Tattoos" in Bibliography);[153] the people made circles on their cheeks with burning wood, and took to other excesses. Fishponds were robbed, taro pulled, pigs killed, and other lawless acts performed."[154]

And Kaumuali'i still lies together with Keōpūolani even now, with also her last husband, Hoapili Ulumaheihei, her daughter with Kamehameha, Nahi'ena'ena, and Hoapili's hānai daughter and one-time O'ahu Governor Kuini Liliha, in the cemetery of the Waiola Congregational Church at Waine'e Street and Shaw Street in Lahaina. These historic ali'i remains were moved there from the Moku'ula ali'i interment site at the order of Bernice Pauahi Bishop in the 1880s. At the Moku'ula site there is now a public park and baseball field. On Kaumuali'i's white memorial obelisk the death date is incorrectly given as "1825," and the only inscription reads "Ka'ahumanu was his wife, 1822 (sic)."

---

[153] See "Tattoos" in Biblio.
[154] Kamakau 1992, p. 266.

KA'AHUMANU IS BAPTIZED AS "ELIZABETH":

After Kaumuali'i's funeral, Ka'ahumanu wanted to be baptized into the Protestant Christian faith, but the Rev. Hiram Bingham refused this because of her marriage to Keali'iahonui, the son of her deceased husband. So Ka'ahumanu released Keali'iahonui from his marriage to her, and was baptized on December 4, 1825 taking the Christian name "Elizabeth" ("Elisabeta").

SON KEALI'IAHONUI'S FATE:

After Ka'ahumanu released him from their marriage, Keali'iahonui converted to Christianity, being baptized as "Arona" (biblical "Aaron," or sometimes "Abner") Keali'iahonui. Described as the "handsomest chief in the islands...and proficient in all athletic exercises," he stayed on O'ahu and married Chiefess Mikahela Kekau'ōnohi, a granddaughter of Kamehameha I and niece of Kamehameha III.

Arona and Mikahela were granted a vast tract of land in Hono'uli'uli around Pearl Harbor on O'ahu...land subsequently so valuable that it be-

Arona (or Aaron or Abner) Keali'iahonui in a late 1840a daguerrotype, from Wikipedia.

came the subject of a notoriously extended land custody case that lasted well into the twentieth century. When Arona Keali'iahonui died at age 48 on 23 June, 1849, the strange disposal of his remains involving a caretaker woman named "Kapule"... a delayed sea committal with two planned human sacrifices stymied...became a case of curiosity for sociologists and psychologists alike.[155]

HIS REBELLION FAILS, BUT "HUMEHUME LIVES":

The matter of the succession to govern Kaua'i and Ni'ihau was finally settled later in 1824 by Kalanimoku and Hoapili Ulumaheihei, who forcefully quelled an armed rebellion against Ka'ahumanu's rule led by Humehume and opposed by Deborah Kapule. Many of the insurgents were killed, their bodies left in the field "to be eaten by pigs" (" 'ai pua'a") including the Chief Kia'imakani who had led the effort to right the *Ha'aheo o Hawai'i*. When Humehume, captured as a "rebel and traitor," was brought before Kalanimoku for judgment, he was surprised to hear Kalanimoku say in Christian charity, "Humehume, live," as he draped an 'ahu'ula cape around his shoulders.[156] The failed rebellion was cause for Kalanimoku to cease his resistance to Ka'ahumanu's desire to

---

[155] See Alexander 1906 at the Hoakalei Cultural Foundation site, also see "Keali'iahonui" and "Kekau'ōnohi."

[156] Warne 2008, p. 202, Del Piano 2009, p. 23.

change the chiefs on Kaua'i, and this replacement of Kaumuali'i's chiefs was immediately begun.

A Portrait of Kalanimoku (1768-1827) by Louis Choris (1795-1828), artist on Russian Captain Kotsebue's ship *Rurik,* 1816. From Wikipedia.

And Humehume did live...in Honolulu exile under the watchful eye of Ka'ahumanu, who gave the name "Wahinekipi" (Rebel Woman) to the daughter that his wife Betty (Pake) had given birth to in November of 1823. But Humehume did not live to see his daughter grow up. He died from "the ha'ole's" influenza on May 3, 1826. His burial place is unknown. His wife and his daughter returned to Betty's adoptive father John Young's home in Kawaihae on Hawai'i island and, after Young's death in 1835, inherited some very valuable plots of land on Hawai'i island and on Maui. I have not discovered the circumstances of her death. By this time the bodies of Liholiho and Kamāmalu, who had died tragically of measles in London, England (she on July 8, 1824, and he, at age 27, on July 14), before they could meet King George IV, had been returned to Hawaii on Lord George Anson Byron's (a cousin of the poet) *HMS Blonde*. Ka'ahumanu, "molder of change," died in 1832, with Kauikeaouli ruling henceforth as "Kamehameha III."

—Lee B. Croft
Phoenix, AZ
April 2017

BIBLIOGRAPHY incuding additional notes:

Alexander, W. D. A Brief History of the Hawaiian People. American Book Company, New York, 1899.

Alexander, W. D. "The Funeral Rites of Prince Keali'iahonui," from the Fourteenth Annual Report of the Hawai'ian Historical Society for the Year Ending December 31, 1906, as included in "The Passing of Keali'iahonui: Burial and Land Case, 1849," on the site of the Hoakalei Cultural Foundation at: http://hoakaleifoundation.org.

Arago, Jacques Etienne. Narrative of a Voyage Around the World, in the Uranie and Physicienne Corvettes, Commanded by Captain Freycinet, During the Years 1817, 1818, 1819, and 1820. Treuttel & Wurtz, Treuttel, jun. & Richter, 1823. Arago is one of the primary artists depicting Hawaiian life in the early contact era. His life is a most fascinating one and his Wikipedia site at http://en.wikipedia.org/wiki/Jacques_Arago provides a link to a French work about curiosities in his travels he wrote while blind in 1853 without once using the the French alphabet letter "a." Curious indeed.

Azambuja, Leo. "The Return of King Kaumuali'i," in For Kaua'i, P.O.Box 956, Waimea, HI, 96796. November 2015, p. 6.

Azambuja, Leo. "Humehume, Kaumuali'i's Lost Son," with art by Evelyn Ritter, in For Kaua'i, P.O.Box 956, Waimea, HI, 96796, Special 2016 magazine edition, pp. 24-29.

Azambuja, Leo. "Chiefess Kamakahelei, Ali'i Nui o Kaua'i," in For Kaua'i, P. O. Box 956, Waimea, HI, 96796, March 2017, pp. 6-7, 4.

Barratt, Glynn. Russia in Pacific Waters, 1725-1825: A Survey of the Origins of Russia's Naval Presence in the North and South Pacific. University of British Columbia Press, Vancouver and London, 1981.

Barratt, Glynn. The Russian Discovery of Hawai'i: The Ethnographic and Historic Record. Editions Limited, Honolulu, HI, 1987.

Barratt, Glynn. The Russian View of Honolulu, 1809-26. Carlton University Press, Toronto, Canada, 1988. See other works of Barratt in Bibliography of Croft 2012 A, B, or C, pp. 325-326.

Barrere, Dorothy B. The King's Mahele: The Awardees and Their Land. Privately published in Volcano, Hawai'i. 1994.

Beaglehole, J. C., ed. The Journals of Captain James Cook. Vol. III, Parts 1 and 2, Hakluyt Society, Cambridge University Press, Cambridge, UK, 1967.

Bealer, Lewis W. "Bouchard in the Islands of the Pacific," in Pacific Historical Review, Vol. 4 (1935), pp. 328-342.

Beckwith, Martha W. "Kauwa" from the Martha Beckwith Collection of Notes, HEN, Vol. 1, 1468-1469. Bishop Museum Archives. Made accessible online through http://www.hawaiialive.org under "Topics." Accessed February 20, 2017.

Beckwith, Martha Warren, ed. Kepelino's Traditions of Hawai'i. Bernice P. Bishop Museum Bulletin 95, Bishop Museum Press, Honolulu, HI. 2007 from the 1932 original.

Bell, Susan N. Unforgettable True Stories of the Kingdom of Hawaii. Press Pacifica, P.O. Box 668, Pearl City, HI, 96782. 1986. ISBN 0-9166-49-8. Most relevant here is Chapter 1 "The Boys From Cornwall," pp. 11-21.

Bingham, Hiram. A Residence of Twenty-one Years in the Sandwich Islands. Charles E. Tuttle, Tokyo, 1981.

Bingham, Sybil. "Journal (1819-1825)." Journal Collection. Hawaiian Mission Children's Society Library, Honolulu.

Boit, John (Edmond Hayes, ed.) Log of the *Union*, John Boit's Remarkable Voyage 1794-1796. Oregon Historical Society, 1981.

Болховитинов, Н. Н. "Русские на Гавайях (1803-1825)" Библиотека/Северная Америка: Век девятнадцатый at america-xix.org.ru. Last accessed January 13, 2017. 45 pp. essay by Nikolai N. Bolkhovitinov of St. Petersburg University, Russia, on "Russians in Hawai'i," including "Авантюра доктора Шеффера (1815-1819) ("The Adventure of Doctor Schaeffer," also see source below).

Bolkhovitinov, N. N. "The Adventure of Doctor Schaeffer on Hawai'i, 1815-1819" in Hawaiian Journal of History, Vol. 7 (1973), pp. 55-70.

Bolkhovitinov, N. N. The Beginnings of Russian-American Relations, 1775-1815. Translated by Elena Levin. Harvard University Press, Cambridge, Massachusetts and London, England. 1975. This work has detailed information about the activities of Alexander Baranov on behalf of the Russian-American Company in Novo-Arkhangelsk (Sitka), Alaska. See others of Bolkhovitinov's Russian works in the Bibliography of Croft 2012 A, B, or C, pp. 329-330.

Burgess, Frank (narrator) and MacGowan, Donnie (producer). "Mo'okini Heiau: Warrior Kings and Human Sacrifice on Hawai'i" posted January 3, 2009 and accessed February 18, 2017 at http://www.tourguidehawaii.blogspot.com.

Bushnell, Andrew F. "The 'Horror" Reconsidered: An Evaluation of the Historical Evidence for Population Decline in Hawaii, 1778-1803." From Pacific Studies, Vol. 16, No. 3 (September 1993), Editor's Forum, pp. 115-183. See Stannard (below).

Buyers, Christopher. "Kauai: Brief History: Genealogy," site accessed February 16, 2017 (posted as copyright Christopher Buyers, August 2000-October 2008) at" http://www.royalark.net/Hawaii/kauai.htm. Such genealogies are very difficult to make and Buyers deserves credit for this one, but he has drawn criticism…see hawaiianlibrarian.wordpress.com for the response of the Mahoe family representative, who also complains of the work at kekoolani.org as well.

Cahill, Emmett. The Life and Times of John Young, Confidant and Advisor to Kamehameha the Great. Island Heritage Publishing, 99-880 Iwaena Street, Aiea, Hawaii, 96701, 1999, ISBN 0-89610-449-4.

Chamisso, Adelbert von. A Voyage Around the World with the Romanzov (sic) Exploring Expedition, 1815-1818. Edited and translated by Henry Katz. University of Hawaii Press, Honolulu, 1986. Chamisso was a noted poet and artist who was about the Russian Navy ship *Rurik* under Captain Otto von Kotsebue who visited Hawaii in 1816.

Chapman, Don (with William Kaihe'ekai Mai'oho, foreword by Palani Vaughn). Mauna Ala: Hawai'i's Royal Mausoleum: Last Remnants of a Lost Kingdom. Mutual Publishing, 1215 Center Street, Suite 210, Honolulu, HI 96816, 2004. ISBN 1-56647-700-X.

Cartwright, Bruce. "The First Discovery of Honolulu Harbor," in Annual Report of the Hawaiian Historical Society For the Year 1922 Vol. 32 (January 25, 1923). pp. 29-37. Detail about the Battle of Kuki'iahu (Mare Amara and Ka'eo).

Chevigny, Hector. Lord of Alaska: Baranov and the Russian Adventure. The Viking Press, New York, 1943. Very colorful.

Choris, Louis (Ludwig or Liudovik). Voyage pittoresque autour du monde. Isles Sandwich. Paris. 1822. This work can be found in antiquarian shops online but is quite expensive. Choris was an artist on Captain Otto von Kotsebue's Russian Navy ship *Rurik* with Chamisso (above). Choris gave us likenesses of Kamehameha and Ka'ahumanu from 1816. He was shot and killed by armed robbers in Mexico in 1828.

Clayton, Jane M. Ships Employed in the South Sea Whale Fishery from Britain: 1775-1815: An Alphabetical List of Ships. Berforts Group. London. 2014. ISBN 978-1908616524. See Howay, Fromm as well on the ships.

Colnett, James. The Journal of Capt. James Colnett Aboard the *Argonaut* from April 26, 1789 to November 3, 1791. Edited by F. W. Howay, Champlain Society, Toronto, Canada, 1940.

Cook, Chris (Editor and contributing author). A Kaua'i Reader: The Exotic Literary Heritage of the Garden Island. Mutual Publishing, 1215 Center Street, Suite 210, Honolulu, HI, 96816. Especially "Kaumuali'i—Kaua'i's Last King" (pp. 78-88). 1995. ISBN 978-1-56647-832-8.

Cordy, Ross. Exalted Sits the Chief: The Ancient History of Hawai'i Island. Mutual Publishing, 1215 Center Street, Suite 210, Honolulu, HI, 96816, copyright 2000. ISBN 1-56647-340-3.

Cordy, Ross. The Rise and Fall of the O'ahu Kingdom. Mutual Publishing, 1215 Center Street, Suite 210, Honolulu, HI, 96816, copyright 2002, ISBN 1-56647-562-7. This work has some mention of earlier habitation dates, but, in the main, correlates the oral historians' genealogies (see Table of Rulers, p. 19 and note 10 on p. 51) for the O'ahu rulers with the scientific dating techniiques, I my judgment affirming their accuracy.

Corney, Peter. Voyages in the North Pacific on the ship Columbia from 1813 to 1818. Reprinted from the 1896 Edition published by Thomas Thrum by Ye Galleon Press, Fairfield, Washington, 1965.

Croft, Lee B. George Anton Schaeffer: Killing Napoleon From the Air. Sphynix Publications, Phoenix, Arizona, 2012(A), ISBN 978-1-105-88437-5.

Croft, Lee B. (with illustrations by Brook Kapūkuniahi Parker). George Anton Schaeffer: Arm Wrestling Kamehameha. Sphynx Publications, Phoenix, Arizona, 2012(B), ISBN 978-0-9858908-1-0.

Croft, Lee B. George Anton Schaeffer: Shipping Germans to Brazil. Sphynx Publications, Phoenix, Arizona, 2012(C), ISBN 978-0-9858908-2-7. See pp. 212-215 when John Marshall tells Dr. Schaeffer about Kaumuali'i's last years in Bremen, Germany, in February 1828.

Crowe, Ellie (illustrated by Don Robinson) Kamehameha: The Boy Who Became a Warrior

King. An Island Heritage Classic, Island Heritage Publishing, 94-411 Kō'aki Street, Waipahu, HI 96797-2806, Fourth printing 2012, ISBN 1-59700-591-6.

DauBach, Daniel Carl. Peter Dobell, 1775-1852: An American Opportunist in Russian Service in Early Nineteenth Century Siberia. University of Kansas Ph.D. Dissertation, 1993. Available through University Microfilm International, 300 Zeeb Road, Ann Arbor, MI 48106-1346 as order number 9425901. The internet presence of this work (accessed in 2010) rephrases the title, replacing the word "Opportunist" with "Huckster." Dobell was from Philadelphia, but disavowed America and claimed to be an Irishman, being named Russian minister to the Philippines after trade activity and anti-pirate activity in Canton. Dobell and George Anton Schaeffer never met, although their trails crossed several times. Dobell was in Manila when it was blockaded by Hypolite Bouchard's 34-gun Frigate *Argentina* in early 1818, and in 1819 on his own ship *Sylph* was in Hawaii and advised Liholiho on breaking the kapus and dealing with his resistant chiefs. Dobell's advice to the Russian government coincided with Dr. Schaeffer's as far as Hawaii was concerned. He advocated a Russian annexation of the islands for advantages of Pacific trade. See more in Croft 2012 B, p.340, also Croft 2012C, pp. 65-111. And see the fine commentary by Mills 2002, pp. 30-32.

Daws, Gavan. Shoal of Time: A History of the Hawaiian Islands. University of Hawaii Press, Honolulu, first printing 1974. ISBN 0-8248-0324-8. A wonderfully readable account throughout without sacrificing accuracy, it set the standard high.

Day, A. Grove. A Biographical Dictionary: History Makers of Hawaii. Mutual Publishing of Honolulu, 2055 King Street, Honolulu, HI 96819. 1st printing, 1984. ISBN 0-935180-09-5.

Day, A. Grove. "Georg Anton Scheffer: Russian Flags Over Hawaii" in Rogues of the South Seas. Foreword by James Michener. Mutual Publishing, Honolulu, 1986. An anecdotal treatment in a popular paperback, but accurate.

Delano, Amasa (1763-1823). This relative of U.S. President Franklin Delano Roosevelt wrote A Narrative of Voyages and Travels Round the World: Together with a Voyage of Survey and Discovery in the Pacific Ocean and Oriental Islands. E.G. House. Boston. 1817. This is the work of the American Revolutionary War hero and "Master Mariner," Amasa Delano, who, after a visit to Kealakekua Bay in 1801 on his ship *Perseverence*, took away with him a son of Kamehameha's who called himself "Alexander Stewart" after an officer on Captain William Brown's *Jackal* who played a role in interisland hostilities on O'ahu in 1794. He and four other kanakas were to be trained as sailors and then educated in the United States for eventual advantageous return (like Kaumuali'i's son Hume-hume). Delano records having these five Hawaiian youths innoculated with "kinepox serum" as they approached Canton, China. Thus a son of Kamehameha's was among the first Hawaiians vaccinated against smallpox. In Canton, this son transferred himself to a British Indiaman (trade ship) and was last heard of in London. See the biography by James Connolly at http://www.delanoye.org/Primary/AmasaXV.html. Delano's adventures also inspired a short story by Herman Melville from 1855 entitled "Benito Cereno." See also the article "Did Kamehameha Have a Lost Son" in http:hawaiiantimemachine.blogspot.com which has Hawaiian history authority Thomas G. Thrum (1842-1932) refuting the contention (from Fornander?) that this son was Pauli Kaoleioku, son of Kamehameha's early wife and high chiefess Kānekapōlei.

Del Piano, Barbara. "Kalanimoku: Iron Cable of the Hawaiian Kingdom, 1769-1827," in The Hawaiian Journal of History, Vol. 43 (2009), pp. 1-28. Now THE work on Kalanimoku, and well illustrated as well. Just a fine fine work.

Desha, Stephen L. Kamehameha and His Warrior Kekūhaupi'o. Translated by Frances N. Frazier. Kamehameha Schools Press, Honolulu, 2000.

Dibble, Sheldon. History of the Sandwich Islands. T.H. & T.G. Thrum. Honolulu, 1909.

Dickey, Judge Lyle A. Touring the Legends of Wailua. Kaua'i Historical Society, P. O. Box 1778, Lihue, HI, 96766, 2014 (as originally presented by Judge Dickey to the KHS in 1915), 32 pp. ISBN 0-9703293-2-6.

Doughty, Andrew. The Ultimate Kauai Guidebook: Kauai Revealed. Wizard Publications Inc., P.O. Box 991, Lihu'e, Hawai'i, 96766-0991, 7th edition, 2011, ISBN 978-0-9814610-1-4.

Dukas, Neil Bernard. A Military History of Sovereign Hawai'i. Mutual Publishing, 1215 Center Street, Suite 210, Honolulu, HI, 96816, 2004. ISBN 1-56647-636-4.

Dukas, Neil Bernard. The Battle of Nu'uanu, 1795: An Illustrated Pocket Guide to the O'ahu Battlefield. Mutual Publishing, Honolulu, HI, 2010. ISBN 978-1-56647-922-6.

Ellis, William. Journal of William Ellis: A Narrative of an 1823 Journey Through Hawai'i, with Remarks on the History, Traditions, Manners, Customs, and Language of the Inhabitants of the Sandwich Islands. Mutual Publishing, 1215 Center Street, Suite 210, Honolulu, HI, 96816, 2004 printing, ISBN 1-56647-605-4.

Fornander, Abraham. Ancient History of the Hawaiian People. Mutual Publishing, 1215 Center Street, Suite 210, Honolulu, HI 96816, 1996.

Fornander, Abraham. Collection of Hawaiian Antiquities and Folk-Lore. (Translated, Edited and Illustrated by Thomas G. Thrum). Third Series. Memoirs of the Bernice Pauahi Bishop Museum, Vol. VI, Bishop Museum Press, Honolulu, H. I., 1919-1920. This volume for two chants of Kaumuali'i, pp. 474-483. Available at Ulukau.org.

Franchere, Gabriel. Narrative of a Voyage to Northwest Coast of America in the Years 1811, 1812, 1813, and 1814 of the First American Settlement on the Pacific. Translated and edited by J. V. Huntington. Redfield. 110 and 112 Nassau Street. New York. 1854. Wonderful detail about life on Kamehameha's Hawai'i.

Fromm, James R. "Early Sailing Ships Trading on the Northwest Coast of America, 1788-1837." at: http://3rd1000.com, last accessed February 4, 2017. A useful work, related to that of Howay (below) and Clayton (above). The descriptions of the various types of ships is valuable to the historians of the wooden sailing vessels of the period.

Fujimoto, Dennis (photo and text?). "Kauai's King Honored," The Garden Island. October 24, 2014. This article mentions that a long-time guide from the West Kaua'i Technology Center in Waimea (and the President of Kaua'i's "Friends of King Kaumuali'i" cf. http://kauaikingkaumuali-i.org) has a piece of tapa that once swaddled a child named Kainoahou, meaning "the sea is free," born ca. 1815 to King Kaumuali'i and a woman "with whom he established a relationship." I conjecture this child to have been male from genealogical evidence from the Sinclair family tree at www.ancestry.com that intersects with my own family tree in the tenth century in Normandy, and from an October 31, 1984 application to the United States Department of the the Interior for a "Historic Places" registration of the "Charles Gay Residence" in Waimea on Kaua'i, wherein a description of the residence's history relates from an interview with a "Roland Gay" from February 10, 1977 that: "Charles Gay married Louise Kala, granddaughter of High Chief *Kainoahou* (Italics mine, author), son of King Kaumuali'i, the last King of Kauai. They had eleven children."

Gast, Ross H. Don Francisco de Paula Marin. with: The Letters and Journal of Francisco de Paula Marin (Edited by Agnes C. Conrad). University Press of Hawaii/The Hawaiian Historical Society, Honolulu, HI 96822, 1973. ISBN 0-945048-09-2.

Golovnin, Vasilii M. (Captain) Around the World on the *Kamchatka*, 1817-1819. Translated from the Russian and with an Introduction and notes by Ella Lury Wiswell (who once taught Russian to the parents of U.S. President Barack Obama, who met in her class). University of Hawaii Press at Manoa, HI, 1979. ISBN 0-8248-0640-9. Memoirs include Golovnin's visit to Hawaii.

Greatheed, Rev. S. "The Manuscript of Rev. S. Greatheed," in The Friend, Honolulu, June 2, 1862. Accessed in February 2017 at http://server2honweb.com/mhm-friend/cgi-bin/mhm-friend. See Massey (below), p. 128, who appraises this source on the 1794-5 role of the ships *Jackal* and *Lee Boo*.

Greer, Richard A. "Along the Old Honolulu Waterfront" in Hawaiian Journal of History (A publication of the Hawaiian Historical Society), Vol. XXXII (1998), pp. 25-66. Good detailed history with included maps from as early as 1810 and others, of Honolulu and environs, with relations of related events and historical developments.

Grigg, Dr. Richard W. In the Beginning—ARCHIPELAGO—The Origin and Discovery of the

Hawaiian Islands. Island Heritage Publishing, 94-411 Kō'aki Street, Waipahu, HI, 96797-2806, 2012. ISBN 1-61710-151-6. See author Lee B. Croft's review of this work on www.amazon.com.

Gutmanis, June. Na Pule Kahiko:Ancient Hawaiian Prayers. (Drawings by Susanne Indich) An Editions Limited Book, P.O.Box 10150, Honolulu, HI, 96186, Copyright 1983, 4th printing. ISBN 0-9607938-6-0. See Chapter IV: "Po'ino, Make, Malu" ("Misfortune, Death, Protection")...p. 24-31.

Handy, E.S. Craighill. Polynesian Religion. Bishop Museum Press, Honolulu, HI, 1927.

Handy, Willowdean Chatterson. Tattooing in the Marquesas. Dover Publications Edition, Mineola, New York, 2008, ISBN 978-0-86-46612-5. This is a reprint of the Bernice P. Bishop Museum publication of 1922.

Hawaii Legal Authority (a non-profit charitable organization comprised of the spouses of the members of the Hawaii State Bar Association). "Kānāwai Māmalohoe" ("Law of the Splintered Paddle"). Illustrated by Dietrich Varez. See at https://www.hawaii.edu/uhelp/files/LawofTheSplinteredPaddle.pdf (last accessed February 4, 2017. This "law," incorporated into the Hawai'ian constitution is: "E nā kānaka,/E mālama 'oukou i ke akūa/A e mālama ho'i i kānaka nui/a me kānaka iki;//E hele ka 'elemakule,/Ka luahine, a me ke kama/A moe i ke ala/'a'ohe mea nāna e ho'opilikia./Hewa nō, make." Translation here is: "O my people,/Honor thy gods;/Respect alike (the rights of)/men great and humble;/See to it that our aged,/ Our women, and our children/Lie down to sleep by the roadside/without fear of harm./Disobey, and die."

Hertz, Robert. "Contribution a une etude sur las representation collectiv de las mort," in Annee sociologique, 10 (1907), pp. 48-137.

Ho'omaka'ikai (Explorations), 4th Edition, 2007, Kamehameha Publishing, 567 S. King Street, Honolulu, HI, 96813.

Ho'omanawanui, Ku'ualoha. "Hahohano Wailuanuiho'āno: Remembering, Recovering, and Writing Place," from Hūlili, Vol. 8 (2012), pp. 190-247. This work focuses on legends, traditions, and people of Kaua'i's ahupua'a of Wailua and includes wonderful details and scholarly discussion. Especially useful on the cultural importance of related Hawai'ian "oli" (chants) and "mele" (songs).

Howard, Cameron B. R. "What's With All the Begats?" on the site, "Everything You Wanted to Know About the Bible But Were Afraid to Ask" at: http://www.enterthebible.org/blog.aspx?

post+2646. Posted August 1, 2013, Accessed February 21, 2017.

Howay, Judge Frederick W. "A List of Trading Vessels in the Maritime Fur Trade," "Part 2" of each of the years 1930-1934 and especially Part 2 of 1932, pp. 43-86 covering the voyages of ships from 1805-1814, *Royal Society of Canada: Transactions*...this is the source, to affirm that Kamehameha and Kaumuali'i negotiated Kaua'i's succession on Captain Nathan Winship's brig *Albatross* in early April of 1810, and also eliminates the *O'Cain* as the site of this historic meeting. Many scholars, in doubt, don't say. This information is also to be seen in Pierce, 1976b, p. 229, 240. See also Pierce, 1990, p. 540: Entry on Nathan Winship for evidence about William Smith being the "hostage mate." On ships see also Fromm and Clayton.

Ii, John Papa (Translated by Mary Kawea Pukui, and edited by Dorothy B. Barrere). Fragments of Hawaiian History as Recorded by John Papa Ii. Bishop Museum Press, Honolulu, HI, 1959.

Jarves, James Jackson. History of the Hawaiian or Sandwich Islands. 3rd edition. Charles Edwin Hitchcock, Honolulu, 1847 (from earlier 1843 Boston edition by Tappan and Dennet).

Joesting, Edward. Kauai: The Separate Kingdom. University of Hawaii Press and Kauai Museum Association, Ltd., 1984, ISBN 0-8248-1162-3.

Kaeppler, Adrienne L. Feather Cloaks, Ship Captains, and Lords. Occasional Papers of Bernice P. Bishop Museum, Honolulu, HI. Vol. XXIV, No. 6, July 8, 1970.

Kalahiki, Mel. "The Story of Ka'iana" at http://pacificworlds.com. Accessed January 20, 2017.

Kalakaua, King David ("His Hawaiian Majesty," edited and with an introduction by Hon. R. M. (Rollin Mallory) Daggett, foreword by Glen Grant). The Legends and Myths of Hawaii. Mutual Publishing, 1215 Center Street, Suite 210, Honolulu, HI, 96816, 1990. ISBN 0-935180-86-9. Especially "The Iron Knife" (pp. 175-205).

Kamakau, Samuel M. Ruling Chiefs of Hawaii. Revised Edition, Kamehameha Schools Press, Honolulu, 1992. ISBN 0-87336-014-1.

Kamakau, Samuel M. Ka Po'e Kahiko: The People of Old. (Translated from the Newspaper Ke Au 'Oko'a by Mary Kawena Pukui, arranged and edited by Dorothy B. Barrere, Illustrated by Joseph Feher). Bernice P. Bishop Museum Special Publication No. 51. Bishop Museum Press, Honolulu. paperback edition, 1964. ISBN 0-930897-81-1.

Kamakau, Samuel M. "Tattooing" From "Ke Au Okoa" March 31, 1870. HEN I: 1289-1291, Bishop Museum Archives. Made accessible at http://www.hawaiialive.org. Accessed February 23, 2017.

Kamakau, Samuel M. "A Man of the Sandwich Islands by John Webber, Half Face Tattooed," from Ke Au Okoa, Buke 5, Helu 51, Apelili, 1870. Made accessible at http://www.hawaiialive.org. Accessed February 22, 2017.

Kame'eleihiwa, Lilikalā. Native Land and Foreign Desires: Pehea Lā E Pono Ai? Bishop Museum Press, Honolulu, HI, 2002, ISBN 0-930897-59-5. The first five chapters are useful here.

Kanakahelela. "Typescript of Lahainaluna Student Composition no. 15: Recollections of Kanakahelela, Information from an old man on fishing grounds, heiaus, legend of Kaumuali'i, caves, etc." from a Hawai'ian oral interview August 2, 1885. Bishop Museum Archives HI.HI07.15. 15 pp. with English translation.

Kāne, Herb Kawainui. Pele, Goddess of Hawai'i's Volcanoes. The Kawainui Press, Captain Cook, Hawaii 96704-0163, copyright 1987 (2000 printing). ISBN 0-943357-01-2.

Kāne, Herb Kawainui. Ancient Hawai'i. (text and illustrations by artist Kane), The Kawainui Press, Captain Cook, HI, 96704-0163, 1997. This book, like the author, is a "treasure of Hawai'i." Let it all enter your mind's eye from here.

Kāne, Herb Kawainui. Voyagers. Published by Whalesong, Inc., A Beyond Words Publishing Company Special Edition. First Edition, September 4th, 1991. ISBN 0-9627095-1-4. Order at P.O. Box 163, Captain Cook, HI 96704.

Kane, Charlotte N. "Descendents of Kaumuali'i (1776 (sic)-1824)" at http://familytreemaker.genealogy.com/users/k/a/n/Charlotte-Kane-HI/PDF-GENE02.pdf . Accessed in April 2009.

Kaua'i moku (districts and auhupua'a) at http://kauainuikuapapa.com and http://islandbreathcom accessed January 20, 2017.

Kawaharada, Dennis. "Hawaiian Human Sacrifice" at: http://2.bp.blogspot.com/_aMoi5cm-V_uQ/TKf6zc8E1Jl/AAAAAAAAAu8/g25b4Pu-X9SU/s1600Goya.jpg. Posted October 2nd, 2010. Accessed February 21, 2017.

Kawaharada, Dennis. "Introduction to The Wind Gourd of La'amaomao," This 1992 discussion of Moses Kuaea Nakuina's 1902 book is available at www.hawaii.edu . I was looking here for references to "Kulepe" as the son of La'amaomao, and also at http://lowchenaustralia.com which has published a "List of Hawaiian Gods and Goddesses."

Keali'iahonui (Christian name "Arona," "Aaron" or sometimes "Abner," he was Kaumuali'i's son by Kapua'amohu and intended heir before the 1810 surrender of his succession to Liholiho). Keali'iahonui has a Wikipedia site with the only known likeness, a historically significant early daguerrotype, at: https://en.wikipedia.org/w/index.php?title=Kealiiahonui&oldid=756537113. The site cites the work here by Bingham, Buyers, and by W.D. Alexander. A family tree at www.geni.com by Tammi Lahela Oberle (posted September 2, 2014) has a likeness of Keali'iahonui's last wife, Kekau'ōnohi (1805-1851). At a family tree on www.ancestry.com can be found a ni'aupi'o marriage of Keali'iahonui not listed elsewhere that I know of to Kinoiki Kekaulike Kaumuali'i…his full sister by Kapua'amohu…resulting in a son named Joseph Kaluakana, with issue through a Maria Pikao of two daughters, Ana Marie Pikao and Leilani Pikao who died in 1984. This is significant because of Kinoiki Kekaulike's known marriage to Kūhiō Kalaniana'ole, from which was born Prince Jonah Kūhiō Kalaniana'ole (1871-1922), Prince of Hawaii and Representative of the Territory of Hawaii to the U.S. Congress from 1903 to his death in 1922. Strange, I think, is that there is a Croatian Wikipedia site (at hr.wikipedia.org) on Kekau'ōnohi with a photograph of her gravesite adjacent to that of Kaumuali'i in the cemetery of the Waiola Congregational Church at Wainee Street and Shaw Street in Lahaina, Maui. Sites accessed February 20, 2017. See also Susanna Moore below.

Kekau'ōnohi (1805-1851). See above entry on Keali'iahonui as well as the English Wikipedia entry https://en.wikipedia.org/wiki/Kekauōnohi, which has a photograph of her, which says that she and Keali'iahonui "had no children." Site accessed February 20, 2017.

Kekoolani, Dean. See his genealogical work at http://kekoolani.org. Accessed in January 2017, I found new information on Kaumuali'i's wife Naluahi...that she was thought to be a granddaughter of Kamehameha's kahuna nui (head priest) Hewahewa, but Kekoolani states that she died in 1895 at age 88 ("nupepa" obit as source?). If this is true, my estimated date of 1803 for her marriage to Kaumuali'i cannot be accurate. Kekoolani also lists a "wife" named "Ni'ihau" as the putative mother of Kaumuali'i's son Humehume, but says clearly that this is unsure. See criticism of this site at hawaiianlibrarian.wordpress.com.

Khlebnikov, Kiril Timofeevich. <u>Baranov: Chief Manager of the Russian Colonies in America.</u> Translated from the Russian by Colin Bearne and

Edited by Richard A. Pierce. The Limestone Press, Kingston, Ontario, Canada. 1973. This is the seminal biographical work on Alexander Baranov by a long-time Russian-American Company employee.

King, Robert J. "John Meares: Dubliner, Naval Officer, Fur Trader, and Would-be Colonizer" at http://www.web.viu.ca. Accessed February 12, 2017. Thorough work with great notes.

Kirch, Patrick Vinton. A Shark Going Inland Is My Chief: The Island Civilization of Ancient Hawai'i. University of California Press, Berkeley and Los Angeles, California and London, England. 2012. ISBN 978-0-520-27330-6. In his review of this book on www.amazon.com author Lee B. Croft writes: "On a scale of 1-10, this book is an 11." Inspiring scholarship.

Klieger, P. Christiaan. Moku'ula: Mau'i's Sacred Island. Bishop Museum Press, 1525 Bernice Street, Honolulu, HI, 96817, 1998, ISBN 1-58178-002-8.

Kusaka, Maryanne. "Na Wahine Kiekie: Chiefess Kamakahelei, Alii nui o Kaua'i, Emma Kauikeolani Napoleon Mahelona Wilcox," Kauai Historical Society Annual Paina publication, 2012. ISBN 0-9703293-77.

Kuykendahl, Ralph S. The Hawaiian Kingdom, Vol. 1 (1778-1854: "Foundation and Transformation"), University of Hawaii Press, Honolulu. 1938.

Kwiatkowski, P. F. With Illustrations by Tom O'o Mehau. The Hawaiian Tattoo. Halona Inc., Kohala, HI, 1996. ISBN 0-9655756-0-8.

Lee, Blanche Kaualua L. A History of Events in the Life of Hawaii's Horticulturist: Don Francisco de Paula Marin (The Unforgettable Spaniard Who Gave Hawaii the First Pineapple). (Illustrated by Joseph Feher) 2002 copyright, printed in Honolulu, HI. ISBN 1-052-027.

Levathes, Louise E. "Kamehameha: Hawaii's Warrior King." Photographs by Steve Raymer and paintings by Herb Kawainui Kane. In National Geographic, Vol. 164, No. 5 (November 1983), pp. 559-599.

Levin, Stephanie Seto. "The Overthrow of the Kapu System in Hawaii." Journal of the Polynesian Society. Vol. 77, No. 4 (December 1968), pp. 402-430.

Linnekin, Jocelyn. Sacred Queens and Women of Consequence: Rank, Gender, and Colonialism in the Hawaiian Islands. University of Michigan Press, Ann Arbor, MI, 1990. ISBN 0-472-06423-1.

Great sourcework with early memoirs and contemporary historians.

Lisiansky, Urey Fedorovich (Iurii...or Yurii). Voyage Round the World in the Years 1803, 1804, 1805, and 1806. This, #42 in the Bibliotheca Australiana series, is a republication of the English version of *Neva* Captain Lisiansky's Russian ship's log, published in St. Petersburg in 1812. It was published by John Booth in London in 1814, and most lately by Da Capo Press (A division of Plenum Publishing Corp, 227 West 17th Street, New York City, NY), 1968.

Lydgate, Rev. J. M. (John Mortimer). "Kaumuali'i: Kaua'i's Last King," in Hawaiian Historical Society's 24th Annual Report for the Year 1915 (1916), pp. 21-43...the first published English biographic treatment.

Lydgate, Rev. J. M. (John Mortimer). "The Defeat of Kamehameha, 1796." In Hawaiian Historical Society's 36th Annual Report for the Year 1927. pp. 28-45.

Makahiki. Search under "Makahiki" at these sites: www.moolelo.com, www.keolamagazine.com, www.heleloa.com and/or www.hawaiihistory.org. All accessed February 15, 2017.

Malo, David (Translated by Nathaniel B. Emerson). Hawaiian Antiquities: Mo'olelo Hawai'i. Bernice P. Bishop Museum, Honolulu, HI. 1997 edition. ISBN 0-910240-15-9.

Manby, Thomas. "Journal of Vancouver's Voyage to the Pacific Ocean," Honolulu Mercury, June 1929, pp. 11-23.

Massey, Raymond A. (with illustration throughout by Raymond A. Massey, and edited by Jean McGarry and Zelda Feldman). Discovery of Hawaii and Honolulu Harbor. Copyright by Raymond A. Massey, 2009, ISBN 978-0-60725-967-1. On the Battle of Kuki'iahu also see http://en.wikipedia.org/wiki/Butterworth_Squadron. Artist Massey gives likenesses of Ka'eo and Kalanikūpule on p. 96…the only likenesses of them I know of.

Mazour, Anatole G. "Doctor Yegor Scheffer: Dreamer of a Russian Empire in the Pacific." in Pacific Historical Review. No. 6 (March 1937), pp. 15-20.

McCoy, Patrick C. "Archeological Research at Fort Elizabeth, Waimea, Kaua'i, Hawaiian Islands," Phase I Department of Anthropology Report 72-7. Bishop Museum, Honolulu, 1972.

McKinzie, Edith Kawelohea. Hawaiian Genealogies, Extracted from Hawaiian Language Newspapers. Institute for Polynesian Studies, Brigham Young University of Hawai'i Campus, La'ie, HI, 1986.

Meares, Captain John. Voyages Made in the Years 1788 and 1789: From China to the Northwest Coast of America. Walter, London, 1790. See also Robert J. King (above).

Mehnert, Klaus. "The Russians in Hawaii: 1804-1819" in University of Hawaii Occasional Paper No. 38, University of Hawaii Bulletin, Vol. 18, No. 6 (April 1939).

Miller, David G. "Ka'iana, the Once Famous 'Prince of Kaua'i'" in The Hawaiian Journal of History, Vol. 22 (1988), pp. 1-19. The best on Ka'iana. Good source work in the notes as well.

Mills, Peter R. Hawai'i's Russian Adventure: A New Look at Old History. University of Hawaii Press, Honolulu, 2002, ISBN 0-8248-2404-0.

Mills, Peter R. "A New View of Kaua'i as 'The Separate Kingdom' after 1810," in The Hawaiian Journal of History (A publication of the Hawaiian Historical Society), Vol. XXX (1996), pp. 91-104. In this article Mills contends with points made in Edward Joesting's Kaua'i: The Separate Kingdom (see above in this Bibliography) about Kaumuali'i and the building of the Russian Fort Elizaveta at

Waimea. An important point argued therein is that Kaumuali'i had already evidenced non-compliance with his 1810 agreement to function as a tributary chief subordinate to Kamehameha before Dr. George Anton Schaeffer's arrival in 1816. This work is very strong on Kaumuali'i's life and times.

Moore, Susanna. "Keali'iahonui: 'Sprightly and beautiful for a Polynesian,'" a July 11, 2015 blog posting accessed on February 6, 2017: http://paradiseofthepacific.wordpress.com. See "Keali'iahonui" above in bibliography.

Morison, Samuel Eliot. "Boston Traders in Hawaiian Islands, 1789-1823," Proceedings of the Massachusetts Historical Society, October 1920, pp. 166-201. Also printed in Boston Recorder, October 25 & October 30, 1920.

Newspapers. Hawaiian at http://nupepa.org. Ulukau Hawaiian Electronic Library. This source gives Hawaiian-language newspapers (e.g. Nupepa Kuokoa) published between 1834-1948. A January 21, 2017 search there under "Kaumuali'i" revealed two important works, one by Samuel Kamakau, on Kaumuali'i's abduction and includes a tripartite "Mele o Kaumuali'i" as well, at Ka Nupepa Kuokoa, "He Mele no Kaumualii, ke Alii o Kauai, i hakuīa e Kamahelei" Buke VII, Helu 14, Honolulu, Apelila 4, 1864. Obituary notices of figures like Kekaiha'akulou and Keali'iahonui are also to be found there.

Neumann, Paul. "Captain Hypolite Bouchard and his Treaty with Kamehameha I," in the "Fifth Annual Report of the Hawaiian Historical Society for 1897, published by Robert Grieve Publishers, Honolulu, 1898.

Nimmo, H. Arlo. "The Cult of Pele in Traditional Hawai'i," Bishop Museum Occasional Papers, Vol. 30 (June 1990), Honolulu, HI, pp. 41-87.

Окун, Семён Бенционович. Царская Россия и Гаваиские Острова. из *Красного Архива* (*The Red Archive*), Петербург, Том 78 (1936), стр. 61-186. Documents here include Dr. George Anton Schaeffer's Russian correspondence, typed extracts of his Russian-American Company reports, and include Kaumuali'i's signed proclamation of Kaua'i's Russian protectorateship.

Parker, Brook Kapūkuniahi."Ka'iana and Kekupuohi" in http://hawaiianatart.com. Accessed January 20, 2017. In the March 2017 oil painting shown on p. 127…notice the framed portrait of Kaumuali'i on the stone wall (see Croft 2012B, p. 242), the European-style sofa, and the Kāhili feather standard. Notice the crowd of people looking in the open window. My identification of those depicted in the painting are: (L-R) Chief

Ko'upikea of Hanapēpē, Chief Kaela (called "Vorontsov" by Dr. Schaeffer, of the north shore), Missionary Samuel Whitney, Missionary Samuel Ruggles, Humehume (Prince George Tamoree), King Kaumuali'i, Chief Kamaholelani (Kaumuali'i's second-in-command), Queen Kekaiha'akulou (later Deborah Kapule), Chief Kahekili Ha'upu (also called Kaiawa, Kekaiha'akulou's father), Kū'ohu (high priest), and the extremely tall Keali'iahonui (Kaumuali'i's son and intended successor and heir). The title of this outstanding work could be "Ka hālāwai ana o ka makua kāne a me ke keiki" ("The Meeting of a Father and his Son").

Pierce, Richard A. Georg Anton Schäffer, Russia's Man in Hawaii, 1815-1817. Limestone Press, Kingston, Ontario, Canada, 1976, ISBN 0-919642-70-5.

Pierce, Richard A. Russia's Hawaiian Adventure, 1815-1817. Limestone Press, Kingston, Ontario, Canada, 1976, ISBN 0-919642-69-1.

Pierce, Richard A. Russian America: A Biographical Dictionary. Alaska History No. 33, Alaska Historical Commission Studies in History No. 132. Limestone Press, Kingston, Ontario, Canada, 1990, ISBN 0-919642-45-4. Useful also in tracing the commercial ships' journeys.

Pukui, Mary Kawena, and E. W. Haertig, M.D., and Catherine A. Lee. Nānā I Ke Kumu: (Look to the Source). Vol. I and Vol. II. Published by Hui Hanai, An auxiliary of the Queen Lili'uokalani Children's Center, 1300 Halona Street, Honolulu, HI, 96817. 1972. A gold mine of Hawaiian cultural traditions and beliefs. ISBN (of Vol. II) 0-9616738-2-6.

Quimby, George I. "Hawaiians in the Fur Trade of North-West America, 1785-1820," in Journal of Pacific History, Vol. 7 (1972), pp. 93-103.

Quimper, Manuel. The Sandwich Islands. (Translated from the Spanish edition of E. Aguado, Madrid, by Clark Lee). Hawaiian Mission Children's Society, Honolulu, 1822.

Rhodes, Diane Lee (with some additions by Linda Wedel Greene). "Overview of Hawaiian History:" Chapter I—"Before the Written Record," and Chapter V—"Changes After the Death of Kamehameha," Pu'ukohala Heiau NHS; Kaloko-Honokohau NHP; Pu'uhonua o Honaunau NHP at "A Cultural History of Three Traditional Hawaiian Sites on the West Coast of Hawai'i Island" at nps.gov. Accessed February 4, 2017.

Ridley, Scott. Morning of Fire: John Kendrick's Daring American Odyssey in the Pacific. William

Morrow, an imprint of HarperCollins Publishers, 2010, ISBN 978-0-06-170012-5.

Roe, Michael, ed. The Journal and Letters of Captain Charles Bishop on the North-West Coast of America, in the Pacific and in New South Wales, 1794-1799. The Hakluyt Society, 1967.

Rose, Roger. Symbols of Sovereignty: Feather Girdles of Tahiti and Hawai'i. Bishop Museum Press, Honolulu, HI, 1978. Concerning Kamehameha's symbolic bestowal on Kaumuali'i of the Kā 'ei kapu o Liloa sash-girdle.

Ruggles, Samuel. "Samuel Ruggles Journal, 1820-1828." Journal Collection. Hawaiian Mission Childrens Society Library, Honolulu.

Russian Fort Elizaveta (Waimea, Kaua'i). See the work of Peter Mills 2002, and the online sites: http://inwanderlust.blog.com (under "Ghost Towns and Lost Cities: Hawaii," then "Fort Elizabeth— The Russian Fort") and Peter H. Hempfling's excellent compendium site http://starforts.com under "Russian Fort Elizabeth." These sites last accessed March 6, 2017.

Самсонов, Александр. "Утерянные земли России: Рысские Гавайи" at Военное Обозрение (topwar.ru). A 30 page article on "Lost Lands of Russia: Russian Hawaii," including pictures of

Kaua'i's Fort Elisabeth and of George Anton Schaeffer.

Schweizer, Niklaus R. A Poet Among Explorers: Chamisso in the South Seas. Herbert Lang Verlag, Bern und Frankfurt/M., 1973, ISBN 3-261 00809-1.

Silverman, Jane L. KAAHUMANU: Molder of Change. Friends of the Judiciary History Center of Hawaii. Honolulu, Hawaii, 1987, ISBN 0-9619234-0-2.

Soboleski, Hank. Thirty-Nine Biographical Stories: History Makers of Kaua'i: Volume One. A compilation in book form, copyright 2003 by Hank Soboleski, of individual stories in a series entitled "History Makers of Kauai" published in Kaua'i's The Garden Island newspaper from 2000 to 2002. This is a concise treasure trove of historical biographies and has a companion compilation as well entitled Twenty Biographical Stories: History Makers of Kaua'i: Volume Two.

Soboleski, Hank. "King Kaumuali'i's Likenesses." The Garden Island. June 15, 2014. Available at http://thegardenisland.com.

Sowell, Teri L. "Spiritual remains: Hawai'ian funerary rituals and the legacy of Robert Hertz" in Journal de la Societe des Oceanistes, 124, annee

2007-1. pp. 84-88. This is a celebration of 100 years since the publication of Robert Hertz's important work on the collective representations of death. The treatment here is of the Hawaiian " 'iwi" ("bones") as death relics preserving "mana" for the descendents and the changes wrought by the Christian missionaries after 1820. Also a concise explanation of the "Ao" ("light") and "Pō" ("darkness") opposition in Polynesian (and Hawaiian) religion as the origin of "mana," from E. S. C. Handy (see above).

Spoehr, Anne Harding. "Prince George Tamoree: Heir Apparent of Kaua'i and Ni'ihau." In The Hawaiian Journal of History. (A Publication of the Hawaiian Historical Society), Vol. XV (1981), pp. 31-49.

Stannard, David E. Before the Horror: The Population of Hawaii on the Eve of Western Contact. Social Science Research Institute, University of Hawaii, Honololu, 1989. See Bushnell (above).

Stauder, Catherine. "George Prince of Hawai'i." In The Hawaiian Journal of History. (A Publication of the Hawaiian Historical Society), Vol. VI (1972), pp. 28-44. This work includes the most published likeness of George Prince Tamoree (Kaumuali'i)...a portrait sketched by Samuel Finley Breese Morse, artist and telegraph inventor son of Prince George's one-time caretaker Jedediah

Morse), and later painted, then made into an engraving in New Haven in 1822 by N. and S. Jocelyn...see Spoehr above for another derivative likeness and note, p. 43.

Stewart, C.S. Journal of a Residence in the Sandwich Islands. University of Hawai'i Press, Honolulu, 1970.

Stokes, John F. G. "Origin of the Condemnation of Captain Cook in Hawaii" (Hawaiian Historical Society Annual Report for 1930), Honolulu, HI.

Tattoos (Kākau). These sources were accessed simply to ascertain which side of Maui ruler Kahekili's body was famously tattooed black (something numerous historians refrain from saying): see above the works of Handy, Kamakau and Kwiatkowski...also "Island Expat's" work entitled "Pahupu: The Tattooed Warriors of Maui," posted 5 February, 2013 at http://www.hawaiiantimemachine.blogspot.com and accessed February 20, 2017; also mention of the "pahupu'u" (half-body tattooed warriors from Maui) in Thomas G. Thrum's translation from Moke Manu entitled "This Land is the Sea's: Traditional Account of an Ancient Hawaiian Prophecy" made accessible online at http://sacred-texts.com. Accessed February 20, 2017. All these sources say it was the RIGHT side of the body, for various interesting reasons having to do with weapons' handedness, light and dark visibility and such. My own previous conjecture that it was the left side came from Captain Vancouver's comment about Kaua'i beachcomber James Coleman, that he was "tattooed with a broad badge over his left shoulder meeting low down on his left side having a left shoulder drape tattoo on his left side. This was similar to the marking of Kahekili's warriors" (reported by Ridley 2010, p. 260). This more indirect observation is now "overruled" in my mind by these other sources. Also, an extract of mentions of Hawaiian tattooing by Captains Cook and King are given (with the title page of the 1785 edition of their work) at http://hawaiialive.org under "tattoos."

Tabrah, Ruth, M. Ni'ihau: The Last Hawaiian Island. Press Pacifica, P.O. Box 47, Kailua, HI, 96734, 1987. ISBN 0-916630-59-5.

Teilhet, Darwin. Russian Flag Over Hawai'i: The Mission of Jeffery Tolamy. Mutual Publishing, Honolulu, HI, 1986. This is an adventure novel about US President Jefferson's "secret agent" in Hawaii..including a fictionalized "Dr. Sheffer" in command of a villainous band of Aleuts. It makes a villain of George Anton Schaeffer. Dramatizations can be revelatory.

TenBruggencate, Jan K. Hawai'i's Pineapple Century: A History of the Crowned Fruit in the Hawaiian Islands. Mutual Publishing, 1215 Center

Street, Suite 210, Honolulu, HI, 96816. 2004. ISBN 1-56647-667-4. This is a fine history of the Hawaiian pineapple industry, attributing the first cultivation of the pineapple in the islands to Don Francisco de Paula Marin (see Gast and Lee, above).

TenBruggencate, Jan. "Royal Treatment From a King," in For Kaua'i, P.O. Box 956, Waimea, HI, 96796. September 2015, pp. 30.

Te Rangi Hiroa (Sir Peter H. Buck). Arts and Crafts of Hawaii. Bernice P. Bishop Museum Special Publication. Bishop Museum Press, 1525 Bernice Street, Honolulu, HI, 96817. 1957 (2003 printing here), ISBN 1-58178-027-3. The ultimate illustrated masterpiece on Hawaiian arts and crafts. See the section on "Helmets," for relevant example, on pp. 231-248 (p. 240 on the "Kaumuali'i helmet")… on sacrificial eye extraction (p. 3), dog meat in the cuisine (p.4), or Hale construction, pp. 75-106…or much much else. A wonder.

Treadwell, John. Narrative of Five Youths From the Sandwich Islands. J. Seymour, New York, 1816.

Tregaskis, Richard. The Warrior King. Falmouth Press, Honolulu, HI, 1973.

Valeri, Valerio. Kingship and Sacrifice: Ritual and Society in Ancient Hawaii. Translated by Paula Wissing. University of Chicago Press, Chicago, Il. 1985.

Vancouver, George. Voyage of Discovery to the North Pacific Ocean and Round the World. Da Capo Press, New York, 1968.

Wailua Falls. This beautiful double-course waterfall (also called "Wai'ehu Falls") of a branch of the Wailua River to Kaua'i's east coast is a major tourist attraction alleged by Wikipedia (source is Andrew Doughty's The Ultimate Kauai Guidebook: Kauai Revealed. Wizard Publications, 2012, p. 75) to be 173 feet in height. Other places state that it is "about 200 feet high." But I have personally estimated the height by an admittedly rough trigonometric method to be about 120 feet...clearly less than the other sources. Still, before I published in 2012 my illustrated story (Croft 2012B, p. 246) about Kaumuali'i jumping from it and surviving, I had considerable compunction about encouraging foolhardy young imitators to attempt it, lest they injure or kill themselves. But now, as of September 3, 2014, that has happened. A daredevil 21-year-old Californian named Shiloh Shahan can be seen on YouTube.com (search for "Leap of faith off a beautiful Waterfall" on http://YouTube.com for the 1.18 minute video...last accessed January 31, 2017) surviving this leap. I timed his fall on the video at 3.38 seconds from the top to the water below. He suffered a concussion and some muscle tears, became unconscious, and was very fortunate to be rescued by a father and daughter who were at the edge of the bottom pool and happened to see him hit the water. Nearby on YouTube's offerings is an August 19, 2015 video (already seen by 1.3 million viewers) of a "Laso Schaller" achieving the "World Record Cliff Jump Record" by leaping 192 feet (almost 60 meters) from a cliff into a natural pool of water and surviving...exceeding 76 miles per hour (123 kmh) of fall velocity at the end, which came in 3.58 seconds.

Warne, Douglas. "George Prince Kaumuali'i: The Forgotten Prince," in The Hawaiian Journal of History (a publication of the Hawaiian Historical Society), Vol. XXXVI (2002), pp. 59-71.

Warne, Douglas (with the collaboration of Holly Kilinahe Coleman and illustrated by Brook Kapūkuniahi Parker). Humehume of Kaua'i: A Boy's Journey to America, an Ali'i's Return. Kamehameha Publishing, Honolulu, 2008, ISBN 978-0-87336-151-4. Just a fine work.

Waterhouse, Stewart. Stewart Waterhouse, historian and experienced caver, had sites pleasantfields.com and luakini.com that are currently, and unfortunately, down. For several years he was composing, with invited help from site visitors, a work on Hawaiian human sacrifice. The work included Hewahewa's important role in the cessation of human sacrifice when the "kapus" were abandoned in 1819-20, including his "apology" for sacrificing humans and also his advice to Kamehameha on the 1810 baby pig strategy to foil possible death prayers against him. I last accessed this work, and contributed in a minor way, in 2013. It's important work in my opinion and deserves publication and access.

Westervelt, W. D. "The Passing of Kamehameha I" in Annual Report of the Hawaiian Historical Society for the year 1922, Vol. 32 (January 25, 1923), pp. 10-29.

Whitney, Mercy. "Journal, Vol. 1, 1821-1827," Journal Collection, Hawaiian Mission Children's Society Library, Honolulu.

Wichman, Frederick B. Nā Pua Ali'i o Kaua'i: Ruling Chiefs of Kaua'i. A Latitude 20 Book of the University of Hawai'i Press, Honolulu, HI, 2003. ISBN 0-8248-2587-X. I differ with Wichman some on genealogy…paternity of Kapua'amohu, for example, and of Keawe…name "Kina" instead of "Kiha"…place of his death…but certainly Wichman is one of the giants on whose shoulders I stand in this relation.

Wichman, Frederick B. Kaua'i: Ancient Place Names and Their Stories. A Latitude 20 Book of the University of Hawai'i Press, Honolulu, HI, 1998. ISBN 0-8248-1943-8.

Wichman, Frederick B. Touring the Legends of the North Shore. Publications Committee of the Kaua'i Historical Society, P.O. Box 1778, Lihue, HI 96766, 2006, 30 pp. ISBN 0-9703293-1-8.

Williams, Julie Stewart (with illustrations by Robin Yoko Racoma) From the Mountains to the Sea: Early Hawaiian Life. Kamehameha Schools Press, 1887 Makuakane Street, Honolulu, HI, 96817, 1997. ISBN0-87336-030-3. Just a clear, concise, useful wonder of a book.

Williams, Julie Stewart (with illustrations by Robin Yoko Burningham). Kamehameha the Great. Kamehameha Schools/Bernice Pauahi Bishop Estate, Community Education Division, Intermediate Reading Program, 1887 Makuakane Street, Honolulu, HI, 96817, 1993 revised edition, ISBN 0-87336-022-2.

Young, Peter T. http://totakeresponsibility.blogspot.com. This wonderful illustrated website is a major Hawaiian historical resource now, created by a life-long Hawaiian historophile, Peter T. Young...otherwise involved in the site www.hookuleana.com. See the topics alphabetically listed under "labels" (e.g. John **H**arbottle). Last accessed January 13, 2017.

Zambucka, Kristin. KAUMUALI'I: KING OF KAUA'I. This is a compilation of "Excerpts from early writers (and a few later ones) on the life and times of Kaumuali'i the King of Kaua'i" published in 1999 by Regina Kawananakoa, ISBN 0-931897-03-3.

Zambucka, Kristin. Kalakaua: Hawaii's Last King. Mana Publishing Co., Box 22525, Honolulu, HI, 96823, Second Edition printing, 2006. ISBN 0-931897-04-1.

Зорин, А. В. "Первоходец Тимофей Никитич (note: this patronymic is "Nikitich" and not "Osipovich" as I wrote in Croft 2012B) Тараканов" (see Pierce 1990, pp. 497-499, especially 499 for source of this error) including the section "Русские на Гавайях" at america-xix.org.ru. An 80 page essay by A. V. Zorin of St. Petersburg University on "Timofei Nikitich Tarakanov—First to trek across" (i.e. Siberia by land from east to west from Sakhalin…not accurate (author LBC)).

TABLE OF CONTENTS

3. Introduction.
4. Acknowledgements.
5. Habitation of Hawaii: Who, Where, When.
9. Civilization: Gods and Kapus.
12. God Kings and Human Sacrificing.
17. Birth Site and Name of Kaumuali'i.
19. Kaumuali'i's Mother and Her Husbands.
21. First Contact...Capt. Cook.
28. The Raising of Kaumuali'i.
35. The Ane'ekapuahi: Praying one to Death.
36. Kaumuali'i Values Education--English.
38. Kaumuali'i's Marriages and Children
41. Rivalry With Keawe--The Promise.
43. Kaumuali'i's Parents Go to War.
45. Inamo'o Becomes Regent.
45. Kaumuali'i's Ane'ekapuahi Revenge.
47. First Marriage--Kapua'amohu.
48. Kamehameha Takes O'ahu: Nu'uanu.
48. Kekupuohi and Death of Ka'iana.
51. Vanquished Sacrificed, Advisors Spared.
52. Kamehameha's 1796 Attempt on Kaua'i.
54. Brother Keawe Takes Command.
55. Mana Leap From Wailua Falls.
57. Kapua'amohu's Choice.
59. Kaumuali'i Becomes Kaua'i's God King.
64. Kamehameha Plans a Second Attack.
65. Rescued by the Squatting Sickness.
66. Kamehameha and Kaumuali'i Negotiate.
67. Kaumuali'i Chooses Peace for Kaua'i.

72.   Kaumuali'i Escapes From O'ahu.
73.   Tranquility and Profitability for Kaua'i.
74.   The Russian Adventure: Dr. Schaeffer.
77.   Ka'ahumanu Gives Dr. Schaeffer Waikīkī.
81.   Dr. Schaeffer Goes to Kaua'i.
81.   The "Friends George."
88.   Tarakanov's Kauwā Family.
88.   Dr. Schaeffer Opposes Human Sacrifices.
96.   Russians' Trouble in Paradise.
101. Friction Becomes Fire.
102. Dr. Schaeffer Flees Hawaii.
106. Kaumuali'i Cooperates, but How?
113. Death of Kamehameha: Great Changes.
114. The Ritual Chaos.
116. Liholiho Succeeds, Kapus Broken.
122. No More God Kings...but Kaumuali'i?
124. Son Humehume Returns with Missionaries.
128. A New Rivalry, as in Day's Past.
129. Father and Son, But Not All the Same.
132. The Hula and Sexual Relations.
136. A Sad Time for Kaumuali'i.
138. Kaumuali'i is Tested.
140. Liholiho Comes to Kaua'i.
141. Kapus Broken on Kaua'i For All to See.
142. Ka'ahumanu and Kalanimoku Come too.
145. A Marriage Proposal?
147. Kekaiha'akulou Becomes Deborah Kapule.
148. Ka'ahumanu Marries the Son Too.
149. Deborah Kapule's Later Life.
150. Humehume Opposes Ka'ahumanu in Kaua'i.
151. Passing of a Christian: Keōpūolani.

154. Liholiho Sails to England.
155. The Ship *Ha'aheo o Hawai'i* is Lost.
157. Kaumuali'i Passes: A Christian Blessing.
161. Ka'ahumanu is Baptized as "Elizabeth."
161. Son Keali'iahonui's Fate.
163. His Rebellion Fails, But Humehume lives.
166. Bibliography Including Annotations.
209. Table of Contents.
212. List of Illustrations.

Here (L-R) are: a clay maquette of the statue of Kaumuali'i, sculptor Saim Caglayan, Hawaiian language and culture professor Keao NeSmith (the model), and Friends of King Kaumuali'i associate Stu Burley. 2016 photo sent by Maureen Fodale.

List of Illustrations

Front Cover: Portrait of Kaumuali'i.
Back Cover: Fort Elizaveta, RAK Flag
Page 2.   Author Lee B. Croft
Page 14.   Jacques Arago's Execution by Club.
Page 15.   Arago's Execution by strangling.
Page 16.   A Map of the Hawaiian Islands.
Page 17.   Kaumuali'i's Birthplace.
Page 23.   Portrait of Captain James Cook.
Page 26.   Death of Captain James Cook.
Page 37.   Portrait of Capt. George Vancouver.
Page 42.   Statue of Kamakahelei.
Page 50.   Ka'iana, a Prince of Kaua'i.
Page 56.   Kaumuali'i's "Mana Leap."
Page 61.   A map of Kaua'i's Mokus.
Page 68.   Sketch of Kamehameha I.
Page 71.   Brook Parker with Mahiole Cap.
Page 74.   Governor Alexander A. Baranov.
Page 76.   Portrait of George Anton Schaeffer.
Page 78.   Portrait of John Young.
Page 80.   Portrait of Ka'ahumanu's Face.
Page 96.   Kekaiha'akulou in honi with Dr.
Page 105. Author Lee B. Croft with cannon.
Page 117. Liholiho (Kamehameha II).
Page 120. Hewahewa burning the Ki'i.
Page 127. Father and Son Reunion.
Page 143. Portrait of Ka'ahumanu.
Page 150. George Prince Tamoree.
Page 152. Sacred Queen Keōpūolani.
Page 159. Author at Kaumuali'i's Grave Site.

Page 162. Son Keali'iahonui" ca. 1845.
Page 164. Portrait of Kalanimoku.
Page 211. Photo of Clay statue maquette.
Page 213. A Bronze Statue of Kaumuali'i.

This is the bronze statue by Kaua'i sculptor Saim Caglayan that the "Friends of King Kaumuali'i" are trying to get the funds to have enlarged and placed on Kaua'i. Photo sent by Maureen Fodale. To donate, see http://kauaikingkaumualii.org.

PAU (End)

www.ingramcontent.com/pod-product-compliance
Lightning Source LLC
Chambersburg PA
CBHW041429300426
44114CB00002B/14